T0146423

Also by Noni Boon

Pebbles in the Pond - Wave 2 - 'It all starts with me'
Success in High Heels - 'The power beneath me'
Manifesting in High Heels - 'The eyes of the Universe'

HOLIFEST

Noni Boon

BALBOA.
PRESS
A DIVISION OF HAY HOUSE

International bestselling author participating in three anthologies.

Scripture taken from the King James Version (KJV) of the Bible.

Balboa Press books may be ordered through booksellers or by contacting:

Balboa Press
A Division of Hay House
1663 Liberty Drive
Bloomington, IN 47403
www.balboapress.com.au
1 (877) 407-4847

Print information available on the last page.

ISBN: 978-1-5043-0541-9 (sc)
ISBN: 978-1-5043-0542-6 (e)

Balboa Press rev. date: 11/24/2016

Holifest©

Holifest is the power and force that
rockets **'manifest'** to **'magnifest'.**
It is an easy process that brings you everything
you want and at the same time improves
you into what you can become.
When you strengthen yourself, the Universe adds to you.
Holifest gives you the creativity, courage, and
confidence you need to achieve incredible
success and start living your best life yet.

*

Noni Boon

This book is dedicated to my husband, Steven Boon,
who has walked with me through every
lonely 'Void' and is living proof
that I need never settle for 'Limits and Less'.
I give humble thanks to my horse and life teacher 'Suave'.
And a special dedication to all the
animals I have loved and lost.
Thank you 'Max' for strengthening in
me the virtue of self-forgiveness.
I love you family, friends, and of course 'you' – my reader.
Thank you Mum for editing with care.

Contents

Introducing Bruce MacLelland

During the 'New Thought Movement' of the 19th Century, Bruce MacLelland made the statement **'you are what you think, not what you think you are'**. Since then there have been many books written and suggestions made to indicate that your thoughts have a 'power of attraction'. Does this mean that when you think good things, you get exactly what you are thinking about? Is this really how it works? If so, why is it that some of the things you want come along the instant you think about them whereas other things continue to move out of reach and feel like they are never going to happen? Or worse still, they don't. There is more to this 'thought force' than meets the eye; or should I say mind? I have been working on attracting things myself for many years with varying results but just recently, after reading Bruce MacLelland's book **'Prosperity Through Thought Force'**, and really testing the process of manifesting, everything finally fell into place. I have now designed a way that totally works. I want to share this with you so that you stop missing out. Forget learning how to 'manifest'; I am going to teach you how to 'magnifest' using my easy two-ingredient recipe and a simple method called **'Holifest'**. At the same time, you are going to develop into your next best magnificent self, move up to what you can become, and begin living your best life yet.

Although it is good to make every effort to become a better person, just for the sake of it, it also happens to be one of the main ingredients in manifesting; and while it will get you half way there, you need to know the other half, and then pull it all together and put it to the test. First, let me tell you a little bit about Bruce MacLelland. In January 1904, Bruce was a poor bookkeeper earning $1,000 per year. He was working under 'inferior men' whom he did not respect and he felt fierce antagonism towards both people and things. He had few friends, poor health, and worked hard to live a life close to poverty. There was nothing indicating a bright future for Bruce and his life was not working out so well. The thought was brought to his attention that developing **'strength of character'** and learning to **'control mental forces'** could help him obtain **'success in life'**. He knew he was onto something and he had nothing to lose so he decided to use his own life as an experiment and work vigorously to cultivate strength of character, constantly suggesting courage, peace, force, and decision. It was a year and a half before any financial improvement was noticed though it was apparent that he was getting stronger every day and changing for the better.

At the end of the first year, Bruce resigned his position, something he would have been way too afraid to do earlier on. He now voluntarily gave it up, knowing and feeling that he would do better. Within twenty-four hours, an offer of $100 per month was received and he accepted. In six months, his salary was advanced to $1,800 per year because he was the right man in the right place; he dared to assume authority and act independently with a successful outcome. Two months later, Bruce's salary was advanced another $50 per month because he conceived and carried out two ideas that netted many thousands of dollars for his employers. At the end of the second year, Bruce resigned and without capital, opened an office for himself. He was given credit for over $20,000. He was given this credit because those who had dealt with him had 'confidence' in his judgement and honesty. They felt the radiations of ability, honesty, and judgement emanating from his mind. They were picking up on his 'positive vibes', increased strength, and newly acquired belief in himself.

Just one year later, Bruce paid back every dollar he owed and was $11,000 in front. According to my inflation calculator, $11,000 in 1960 is equivalent to roughly $88,495.74 today. Considering that it cost $15 to buy a very good riding horse that would now cost around $15,000, $11,000 was quite an achievement and could afford him to quit the business and pursue his writing. He had plenty of money for all his needs and wants, a happy home, and everything he could wish for but he still had moments of depression, loss of confidence in himself, and lack of faith in God, as well as the occasional inability to sustain a happy buoyance and contentment of mind. Then a reaction would come and he would regain strength to calmly wait to be led, strong in his belief of a guiding hand. I found it reassuring to read that I am not the only person who dips in spirit, loses faith, and flattens out every now and again. This highlights the fact that to be human is to have ups and downs. No matter how good things are, you cannot be 'chirpy' all the time. It is common to feel blue at times, lose confidence, and question your faith. I have discovered however that these moments do not last as long and are much easier to endure when you build 'strength of character'.

Bruce began writing 'Prosperity Through Thought Force' three years before he completed it for the benefit of retrospection. He wanted to test his 'method' and track the results. Following this, he spent the remainder of his life writing, reading, ploughing the fields, riding after cattle, making hay, harvesting corn and cotton, oats and alfalfa, and attending the country fair. It sounds to me like he lived a pretty good life. Although he had plenty of money, he had no intention of spending his life focused on amassing a fortune. He thought this would be 'missing out on fun'. Bruce believed that **contentment and aspiration, coupled with plenty of work brings success**. He said that *"men who seek happiness in travel, in society, in the pursuit of happiness are miserable. The world is full of people who are wealthy and fairly wild with longing for some aim. They do not know what is wrong, and remain miserable. Those who are centering their attention on some work, saving some money, and can see progress in the future, are happy.* ***Success then, is the possession of happiness and a contentment that satisfies the soul"***. In other words, there is no point to being financially wealthy yet soulfully poor and longing for some purpose in life. Although many people look to be successful, and perhaps they are in some areas, true success, absolute success, is obtained by experiencing the serenity of your soul.

Bruce said *"we are only here once, at least that's all we know of now. Let's get money enough, then look around a bit and see what people and things are like"*. Bruce wrote 'Prosperity Through Thought Force' because he could not get it off his mind until it was written. He also said ***"there are many things omitted which should have been included. They may be given to you later"***. I am confident that I know what things have been omitted and I am going to give them to you now. I want to complete the circle and add what Bruce did not include back in 1907. He laid the foundation and wrote a book that gratified his desire to tell others what had been of benefit to him. Like Bruce, I couldn't get this book off my mind until it was written. I had to share with you what has been beneficial to me. I am writing this book to build on Bruce's foundation and take over the reins. I may also 'omit' through my own limited wisdom, and you too will write your chapters. Bruce said *"the exhilaration of freedom reaches its acme of perfection when, **on a good horse**, we fly across the prairies"*. He was right, perfection is found in the exhilaration of freedom. As a horsewoman, this spoke to me. As a writer and counsellor/coach, I followed my soul and answered the call of inspiration to share what I know. As a graphic designer, I have spent years working with the creative process and the universal principles of creation. Bruce said *"It is a psychic law that, to receive, one must first give out"*. **Holifest** is my giving out and I trust that it benefits you as much as it has benefitted me.

Introducing Holifest

Ideas and instructions around manifesting will tell you to work with the 'law of attraction' to create the perfect life and bring forth every alluring want and desire. There are many suggestions out there on how to use this 'universal law' to manifest cars, holidays, jobs, homes, and even relationships. So why is it that this 'process' works for some people and not for others? I couldn't help notice that the word manifest contains the word **'if'** in it – man**if**est. Through my experiments and experience, I have observed that it only works 'if' certain circumstances and conditions come together and align to make it possible; 'if' you have your heart on board, and 'if' it serves your higher good and soul function along with many other pesky 'ifs'. Taking all of this into account, I have designed an effective, accurate, and holistic way to manifest. I have tested it and I know it works. For one, I manifested you reading this book for which I am truly grateful. Let me teach you how to do the same. First you will need some ingredients and an easy to follow recipe. If you are like me, you skip past recipes that have too many ingredients and complicated methods so I am going to keep this as simple and easy as possible.

'Holifest' is abbreviated from 'holistic-manifest'. After studying Holistic Counselling for three years, I know the importance of observing and considering people and life holistically. By this I mean 'whole' – mind, body, and spirit. The concept of holism is that the whole is more than merely the sum of its parts. To ignore one aspect is to dismiss one third of what and who you are. Manifesting requires a holistic process and only works 'if' certain areas of thinking, feeling, and 'being' are addressed. The Universe is aware that you are not just a mind, a personality or an identity. You are also a body and a soul. This is why the methods I have been using to manifest have not been working effectively or consistently. They are too 'thought' and 'mind' oriented and 'omit' the fact that there are three dimensions that make up the all-round (holistic) aspect of being human. A deeper understanding of this 'truth' is what Bruce omitted from his book although he briefly makes reference to his spirit, his soul, and his God. All three aspects of who you are exist and influence each other and one cannot operate adequately without the cooperation and engagement of the other. We constantly interact with objects that have three dimensions – height, width, and depth, and you are no different. Your mind gives you height, your heart gives you width, and your soul gives you depth. To productively 'Holifest', you will need to take a look at some areas of yourself you did not know existed and others you have ignored, neglected, and let slip in thinking that it doesn't matter, doesn't count, or doesn't require your attention.

As promised, the ingredients list is short. In fact, there are only two essential ingredients – **'Strength of character'** and **'Knowledge of self'**. 'Strength of character' is built on a list of twenty-one specifically chosen **'virtues'** that you will discover and develop in yourself. These virtues will strengthen your mind, heart, and soul. They are – **imagination, strength, acceptance, compassion, motivation, detachment, patience, commitment, ethical, excellence, faith, justice, resilience, cleanliness, assertiveness, determination, self-discipline, humility, encouragement, wisdom, and true-gratitude.** 'Knowledge of self' comes through gaining a more 'open' and 'thorough' understanding of your 'holistic self' – mind, body, and soul. Not many cooking recipes have only two ingredients yet I found one – **'Two Ingredient Pancakes'** made from 'mashed bananas' and 'eggs'. The recipe to Holifest is similar in that you have to ripen; mash, and crack open a few things and then follow a very simple 'method'. I have used this cooking analogy because it will help you to form a picture in your mind and make this concept easier to comprehend and relate to. Great teachers throughout history taught through story telling and analogies because people understood them more fully. I will tune you into seeing Holifest through the familiar concept of cooking. Even if you do not cook, I am sure you could knock up some easy banana pancakes (recipe included at the end of the book). William Arthur Ward said *"The mediocre teacher tells. The good teacher explains. The superior teacher demonstrates. The great teacher inspires"*. My intention is to inspire you to know that you already have all that it takes to step into your next best moment in life, and at the same time, improve into 'what you can become'.

The first step to Holifest is to peel the bananas and pull the strings off a few fears and worries, especially the ones that harass you and haunt your peace of mind. Do you find yourself worrying about the future? About things that could happen if it were to all go amiss? Do you feel anxious about losing what you have or not getting what you want? Do you catch yourself going over past upsets or rehearsing for future ones? Do you stress out and then worry about your health? Do you find yourself in 'no win' situations or caught between a rock and a hard place? These situations, thoughts, and worries are all poppycock. Building and adding to your virtues will help you to stop negativity in its tracks and know exactly what to do next. Your worrying thoughts will transform as they are gently replaced with 'strength of character'. I have developed for you a special 'mantra' based on virtues that I encourage you to start using straight away. It goes like this: **'I am creative, courageous, confident, successful'**. Even if you already define yourself as creative, courageous, confident, and successful, there is room for improvement in everyone and life will present you with situations, circumstances, and events that test your resolve in all of these areas. I urge you to say this mantra as often as possible. Say it out loud. Say it with certainty, poise, and fierce expectation. Write it on your arm. Stick it on the fridge. Post it everywhere, tattoo it on your mind, embed it in your heart, and summon it with your soul. The next time someone or something challenges you, say the mantra, and keep saying it until things begin to change.

This mantra is not just a few nice words that I put together on a whim. Firstly, it is entirely purposeful in that it is directed at and calls to your mind, body, and soul individually. Secondly, it strengthens and reinforces you because lingering in a state of mind increases that state of mind. Over time, you will say it, feel it, and become it. Your thoughts become your words, your words become your beliefs, and your beliefs become the foundation of who you are. If you think you are creative, courageous, confident, and successful, you will become just that. Bruce MacLelland said *"All good things come to those who have built up **purity** and **strength of character**"*. He was right. If your first priority is to build strength of character and improve yourself into what you can become, everything else will be added to you and your life will change in ways you could never have imagined.

This means that when you add to yourself, the Universe will add even more to you provided you seek the kingdom of 'God', which is to become more 'virtuous' by developing strength of character. Increasing your virtues takes 'will power' and I will teach you how to access your will. Of course this will take some effort and it asks you to 'step-up', but think about it this way, if you don't make these changes, you will remain trapped in not having what you want and being held back by your frustrations, fears, doubts, and helplessness. If you are reading this book then I suspect you do not want to live your life like this, or perhaps your life is already great but a part of you whispers for something more. One thing I know for certain is that everybody 'wants' something and nobody has reached the absolute. You cannot avoid things going 'wrong' for you. That's life. Every issue, event, circumstance, challenge, or difficulty that comes along in your life has a perfectly matching virtue that you can focus on and strengthen to get you through.

It is a comfort to know there is a simple way to cope with difficulties while improving and adding to yourself. You do not have to go to college or enrol in university to initiate some self-growth and build on your character. You currently possess everything you need in its basic form. Virtues already exist in you and you are already virtuous but you will become more so. Virtues are inherent. They reside in your mind, heart, and soul. They are attributes that are dormant unless struggles and challenges come along to wake them up, and like bananas, they are green unless you ripen them. Your life has and will continue to provide 'opportunities' for you to grow and develop your virtues. Every annoyance, demand, and difficulty is an opportunity. The best way to identify the virtues you most need to build on is to go straight to the people, situations, and circumstances that P you off the most. The Universe has an amazing way of sending you everything you need, often in the form of someone or something you cannot escape. You will be assigned a difficult boss, a narcissistic sister, a demanding partner, a troublesome child, a rotten in-law, a hostile neighbour, a critical associate, or something similar. Alongside this, you will encounter situations, circumstances, and events that provoke, hurt, and displease you. Each one will come with its own 'invitation' to attend with a virtue. When you encounter difficulty, you can choose a virtue from my list of twenty-one and say – "I am (add the virtue)" or you can create a clever little mantra using one or more virtues. I like my friend Jayne's mantra for the virtue of 'acceptance'. She has added a few words and created a rhyme. *"This is where I'm at and I'm accepting of that"*. Create your own mantras for the struggles and challenges you are faced with next.

For example, being asked to re-write a report will invite patience. Lacking energy to deal with your partner will invite commitment. Rebuilding or fixing something for the second time will invite self-discipline. Losing a loved one or suffering a disability will invite acceptance. Standing up to criticism or saying 'no' will invite assertiveness. Every challenging person or event is an iron in the fire of 'strength of character'. When you next feel frustrated, cornered, overwhelmed, or afraid, stop yourself and ask what it is you are dreading and what virtue you need to augment. This will give you your first clue as to where the black spots are in your life. Holifest is an inside job. Start living from the inside out, not the other way around. **When you change yourself, you change your world.** It is as easy as that. Unfortunately it is not enough to just be a nice person and keep your head down, although being nice certainly helps. Building character will ensure that you hold your head high and walk with a spring in your step.

The shape of your body and your posture can tell you a lot about where you are at right now. I have always been round-shouldered and a bit 'slouchy' however when I say the mantra, I straighten up and feel physically stronger and more self-assured. To Holifest, you need purity, strength, and power. You need character, heart, and soul. The Universe upholds a 'law of vibration' whereby 'like attracts like'. Everything vibrates at a certain frequency and attracts to it more that vibrates the same. When you build strength of character, you begin to vibrate at a higher level and you will attract more positive, vibrant people and experiences into your zone. Just 'knowing' that you have virtues is not going to get you there, you have to 'choose' to improve them and remain 'watchful' of your negative states of mind. You must believe in your character and personality and appreciate your own grand uniqueness. You have more going for you than you realise and more potential than you can imagine. Begin by enhancing and building on what you already have. The next time you have a worrying thought, say the mantra. Your inner-Professor of Worry is a persistent, dominating kind of guy who is also a wonderful teacher. He likes to boss you around and scare you into clinging to the wall but he also shows you what you need to build on and he will absolutely fail you if you hand in an assignment on weak virtues.

The next time you fear something that has not yet happened, say the mantra. The next time you are faced with a difficulty or challenge, say the mantra. Keep saying it over and over. Develop your own little tune and sing it. Say it until it forms its own neurological wire through your brain and becomes ingrained in your very being. Think of it as the antidote to fear, anxiety, worry, and stress. This mantra is going to become a very big part of you. It is your new best friend. It is going to become you and you are going to become it. It is going to shape you into your next best magnificent self and launch you toward what you can become. It is going to giddy-up your Holifest and ensures your magnifest. It is the bedrock of Holifest and even if you stopped right here and just adopted this one new habit, your life would change for the better. Say it now and reflect on how it makes you feel ... **"I am creative, courageous, confident, successful"**. Straighten your back and lift your head high. Things are about to change. Do you believe it in your heart? If you do not, you soon will, and if you do, great, the next step is to fold it into your soul.

Do the Shadow Dance

It is time to ripen your bananas for 'Two Ingredient Pancakes'. Fears, doubts, and annoyances are what I call 'shadow virtues'. They are the direct and equal 'opposite' of the character building virtues listed previously. For example, shadow virtues include – laziness, guilt, denial, non-commitment, weakness, lack of faith, arrogance, aggression, judgement, temper, attachment, neediness, hate, non-forgiveness, and self-doubt, just to name a few. Once you ripen these shadow virtues, you can use them to your advantage. You do not want to throw the bananas out. You need them, just as you need your shadow virtues. Your shadow is a part of you that you probably haven't met because most people 'project' their shadow onto other people. Your ego finds it much easier to see fault in others and then tell you that you are not the tiniest bit like that. Your shadow must be recognised in you, not pointed out in other people. You become engaged with your shadow when you think a 'bad' thought. A bad thought could be something mean, cruel, nasty, disempowering, fearful, revengeful, dishonest, or disrespectful. Your shadow is like a tempting little 'devil' that lives in your psyche. It will shock you and not even look back. It will disgust you at times and make you question who you are. It will make you ashamed of what you just thought and not even blink an eye. Do not fret we all have one. You cannot light up a dark room unless you have a dark room to illuminate and standing out in the hallway with a torch will not do it. You have to enter. You have to face your shadow, own it, and then you can add the light by becoming 'whole'.

If you get to know your whole self, your shadow virtues will not need to find another dance partner. If you dance with your shadow, it will not sneak out when you least expect it and express itself through shadow emotions such as anger, insecurity, impatience, criticism, resentment, jealousy, revenge, or rage. Most people do not want to partner up with their shadow. It is understandable that you want the world to see you in your best light. Why would you want to expose yourself and display your 'worst' qualities and characteristics? The truth is, there are some great aspects of you that you cast away to the shadow side of your psyche. I now know that I put 'rebellion' and 'counter culture' way over there when it was not accepted or tolerated by my family, school teachers, or friends. I have since yanked it straight back out and now it helps me to question everything with a healthy sense of scepticism and motivates me to research and make decisions for myself. I am not about to let anyone or anything control me or tell me what to do and my shadow rebel would not let that happen on her watch. What have you tossed away thinking that it is a bad part of you or because somebody else disapproved? What have you separated out into good and bad? What characteristics have been slung aside to make way for the 'acceptable', society fit, more likeable 'you'?

Do not be ashamed of any part of yourself. I am not suggesting that now is the time to start acting out your primal urges but they do serve a purpose or at least they did when you lived in a cave. Your mind is a fascinating dwelling to explore and you can do this by paying attention to what thoughts knock at the door. Become 'whole' and open the door to welcome your shadow virtues, do not chastise them. They are an essential part of you. When I was trying my desperate best to manifest using positive thoughts, affirmations, vision boards and all sorts of other exotic 'tools' that I shook, rubbed, polished, and shoved under my pillow, I developed a strong aversion to my shadow virtues. I felt that they stood in the way and held me back. When I had a negative, judgemental, disempowering, fearful, nasty, pessimistic, frustrated, whining, or moaning thought, I would notice it immediately because I started feeling desperately flat. I sometimes felt like the biggest loser or the worst human being on the planet. You would not believe some of the things I said to myself. I then felt worse when I berated myself for berating myself, knowing it was doing me no good and sabotaging my manifesting process. I was caught in a nasty cycle of negativity and self-annoyance. It was not surprising that nothing I wanted was happening or coming to me. I was painfully aware that I was doing it all wrong but I knew no other way.

This dead end process got me thinking about my psychology study and the actual benefits of the 'shadow'. Perhaps I did not have to get so frustrated with myself after all. Maybe my negative thoughts were a 'message', or a gift. I went hunting through my cupboard for a small book I bought in a second hand bookstore many years ago titled 'Owning Your Own Shadow' by Robert A. Johnson. I re-read the book and the penny dropped. I refreshed my memory on the 'necessity' of the shadow and the importance of seizing it so that you do not live in a state of 'dividedness'. Your shadow keeps your psyche equilibrium. Too much 'goodness' breeds an equal amount of 'badass'. Have you ever noticed how the church elder steals money or how the 'squeaky-clean' teacher moonlights as a sex worker or has an affair with the parent of a student? (This actually happened.) These people have not 'danced' with their shadow and so it sneaks out and becomes unmanageable, unruly, and self-sabotaging. You actually need shadow virtues to be able to have virtues at all. One cannot exist without the other in the same way that hot cannot exist without cold, or night without day.

All negative thoughts serve a special purpose. They alert you to what you need to strengthen and improve. Robert says in his book, *'the balance of light and dark is ultimately possible— and bearable.* ***All nature lives in polarity****—light and dark, creation and destruction, up and down, male and female. It is not surprising to find the same basic laws functioning in our psychological structure'.* Thank goodness we can stop trying so hard to have 'only' positive thoughts and think 'only' nice things. Seize the negative and the nasty just do not act on them, use them to point the way. Exercise your negativity in the same way your immune system brings your body back to health so that it ultimately becomes stronger. You will not build muscle unless you lift a dumbbell. You will not build character unless you lift some shadow virtues. Give your negative thoughts a three-minute rule. Allow three minutes to have a little pity party and then send in the clown. It is necessary for your mind and body to process a balancing amount of negativity. It is not healthy or achievable to 'think positive' all the time. Eckhart Tolle says *'There is an unseen force that causes us to unconsciously seek pain over and over again. Of course no one would do this consciously. No one likes to suffer. And yet we unconsciously create repetitive and unnecessary conflicts. These self-destructive habit patterns are known as the* **Pain Body***. It is a powerful unconscious force with great momentum. Its purpose is to continue the pattern – to bring us pain'*. This is why you have 'downers' just when you were feeling awesome. It doesn't take long before the next thing comes along to P you off and knock you down. A part of you actually 'wants' and 'needs' this to happen for equilibrium, learning, and strengthening.

Eckhart Tolle describes the pain body as a 'psychic parasite' that possesses you and causes suffering. The ego craves pain for equilibrium, stability, and order. Women have this all wrapped up with menstruation. Every month, we feel like crap and our hormones run over us like a bus. Exercise helps pick you up when you are in a funk. Even a walk in fresh air can brighten your mood. If negativity keeps pestering you, choose the virtue of 'acceptance' and let it be until it has done its dance with you. Forcing and resisting is not the answer. A hungry pain body can cause all sorts of trouble. Gently feed it the mantra – 'I am creative, courageous, confident, successful' and fatten it up on a rich diet of virtues. There is a perfect virtue for every situation, circumstance, and event in life. I am a little embarrassed to admit that I have spent my life being afraid to sleep alone in the house, especially now that I live in the middle of the bush and surrounding homes are a fair distance away. Two nights ago, I was lying in bed, one eye open, listening to every noise, imagining a large murderous man in a balaclava with a sharp kitchen knife coming for me. I know that logically this is ridiculous but I was up against the power of unconquered childhood fear and my pain body loves the taste of terror. I tried something new. I created a mantra using a slight variation to annihilate my imaginary intruder. I repeated in my mind "I am courageous and safe. I am courageous and safe. I am courageous and safe".

I said it over and over until I stopped hearing noises, calmed my breath, and gently fell asleep. I was able to affirm it when I woke the next morning without a single stab wound. I have used a mantra to meet every negative, fearful, pessimistic, judgemental, self-destructive, self-loathing or other-person-loathing thought ever since. It works every time. Not some of the time, but every time, with accuracy and certainty. Something mysterious takes place, something shifts, universal magic happens, and without any further effort, I slowly but surely become the mantra and build the virtue. There have been times when I have needed a lot of will power to bring the mantra to the front row of my thoughts. Negativity likes a dress circle seat, not a seat in the gallery. Say the mantra, send your negativity to the back row, and as the colloquialism goes let 'the fat lady sing' her operatic solo of virtues. Manifestation processes suggest ignoring negative thoughts and choosing only positive ones. I am suggesting you welcome and 'use' the negative thoughts to choose a 'virtue', add to yourself, and build character and strength. If a shadow virtue such as intolerance, hopelessness, fear, de-motivation, impatience, dishonesty, or disbelief pops into your mind from your unconscious, you have absolutely no control over that. You cannot choose the thoughts that knock at the door of your mind and let themselves in with or without your permission. They barge in randomly from a place you do not even know exists until you go to sleep and enter the dream state.

Become aware of pessimistic, unfavourable thoughts and use them as a guide. Let's be real, you are going to get the thought equivalent of 'green bananas'. You will never eliminate negative thoughts but you can 'ripen' them ready to use. The next time a shadow virtue tries to trample you, simply ripen it by shining the light on the virtue that is its polar opposite. For example, when you have a 'fearful' thought, choose the virtue of 'courage', and say to yourself – "I am courageous". When you have a 'couldn't be bothered' thought, choose the virtue of 'motivation' and say to yourself – "I am motivated". When you have a 'cannot stand her' thought, choose the virtue of 'compassion' and say to yourself – "I am compassionate". When you have a 'going to kill him' thought, choose the virtue of 'patience' and say to yourself – "I am patient". There is a virtue to match each and every negative thought that shows up. Let's imagine you think about doing something slightly dishonest. Maybe it is the temptation to tell a lie, avoid a conflict, or omit some pertinent details when you really need to be honest and tactful. Simply choose the virtue 'ethical' and say to yourself – "I am ethical". You think ethically, you feel ethical, and you pray to become more ethical. Being ethical will instantly grow in you. This process is immediate. As soon as you think it, you become it and the more you think it, the more you become it. Pray for the ethical virtue and then take it through your mind, body, and soul by thinking it, feeling it, and knowing you already have it.

When you pray for virtues, they are instantly received. It is the same when you pray for help for yourself or another person. However this is not the case when you pray for money, a job, a car, or something else from the material world. The Universe has no delay in delivering virtues and help. It is a language the Universe understands and a wish it is keen to command. The Supreme Intelligence, of which you are a part, has a 'will' that is known as 'God's will'. It says in the modern Lord's Prayer: *your kingdom come, your will be done, on earth as in heaven*. In other words, we are here on earth to do God's will, which is to 'love'. Love flows to you constantly and is expressed through your virtues. It is God's will and God's glory to have the beauty and strength of virtues 'glorified' in you. You need only ask once for a virtue and it is given immediately. The best way you can add to your virtues is to say "I am" and then add the name of the virtue you choose to be more of. 'I am' statements are the most powerful announcements you can make, especially when you think it, say it, feel it, and know it.

The best way to determine which virtues to concentrate on building each day is to notice your shadow virtue via your next negative thought and identify the virtue that matches your next challenge, situation, or event. Bless the negativity. It is the great gift of your shadow. It draws your attention to the need for light and love. When a negative thought comes in, know that it stems from a shadow virtue. If you happen to notice unattractive or inappropriate behaviour in other people, you can use that as a prompt to develop the virtue in yourself. Remember, we are all created from the same 'base'. There is nothing that exists in another person that you do not also have in yourself. People I have taught resist this idea and tell me they could never hurt somebody or murder for example. I then ask what they might do if somebody who had the intention to murder them was threatening their life or the life of someone they love? You do not know what you would do unless you are put in the situation or circumstance that requires a certain behavioural response. Everybody has darkness in them in the form of a shadow. You have become 'socialised' and have learnt to 'control' your shadow whereas people with some mental illnesses do not have that capability. If you witness impatience or intolerance in another, know that you too can be impatient and intolerant and then begin saying the mantra. "I am patient". If you see somebody being angry or aggressive instead of being calm and assertive, do not criticise or confront him or her unless you need to protect yourself, just quietly whisper in your mind – "I am assertive", and you will become more assertive, and perhaps they will too, especially if you pray for them to be.

Holifest will not only bring you abundance, it is also essential for your wellbeing. Anxiety and depression are on the rise along with other 'labelled' disorders. It is estimated that

45% of people will experience a mental health condition in their lifetime. In any one year, one million Australian adults will suffer depression, and two million will suffer anxiety. Almost one in ten women will suffer postnatal depression and at least seven people will take their own life today. These are pretty sobering facts. This subject is close to my heart because I have children who were 'labelled' by Psychologists and Psychiatrists. This was at a time when I did not have the knowledge, tools, and skills that I have today. I followed Doctor's orders and medicated so that they would 'conform' and learn along with the masses. If I had my time over again, I would do things so differently. I now have a more educated understanding of how important it is to eat well, think well, and be well. Although our ancestors did not have the inclination to bask in good memories because they had to prepare for disaster, we do not have to live that way any more. It is pretty unlikely that a sharp tooth tiger is going to take you out on the way to the bus stop. You have to change your inherited mental wiring and optimise the positives. What is the alternative? You can choose between a 'vicious' cycle or a 'virtuous' cycle.

Two Ingredient Pancakes
(the recipe for Holifest)

Ingredient One

• **Bananas**

Ripen your virtues

Ralph Waldo Emerson said *"Our chief want is someone who will inspire us to be **what we know we could be"**.* You are going to become a more creative, courageous, confident and successful 'you'. There is no limit to what you 'could be'. This will be achieved by increasing your strength of character, strength of heart, and strength of soul. Character is built on virtues. You are going to grow your virtues into what you could become starting with what you are going to be next. Virtues are attributes. They make up the 'excellence' of a person and magnify your quality of personality, spirit, and soul. A virtuous person has a strong, dynamic 'character'. Virtuous people are honest, creative, courageous, confident, respectful, forgiving, kind, and generous. Driven by virtues, these people are committed to doing the right thing even

1

when there is a personal cost involved or it is detrimental to them. They have high morals, ethics, and values. They have a personal honour code that cannot and will not be bent or broken. They do not give in to temptation, urges or provocation. They act according to high principles, beliefs, and integrity. You may already be virtuous, but there is room for improvement in everyone. Your virtues need to be cultivated and enhanced in order to Holifest and access more abundance, fulfillment, peace, and happiness. Increasing your virtues builds character, which is one of the main ingredients for Holifest.

Holifest is the key to success. Success is reached when you acquire what is missing in your life and when you achieve what you determine to be your own personal success. Success is different for everyone and falls under different categories such as having fulfilling loving relationships, reaching personal and financial goals, acquiring inner peace, growing in wisdom, having more time and space, or achieving meaningful acquirements. When you gain success through building strength of character and becoming more virtuous, you will start to see results in your life that weren't there before. People will respond to you differently. Your friends, co-workers, family, and associates will develop trust and reliance on you. They will come to you for help, advice, and guidance. You will inspire people to become better because your character will motivate and influence them into doing so. You will be known as a person with exceptional charm, charisma, and personal power. You will no longer find yourself tempted to complain, moan, or bitch about other people, misfortunes, circumstances, or events.

You will have more zest for living and you will vibrate at a higher frequency than before. You will be devoid of drama and you will attract other high quality, virtuous people to you. You will notice some people 'drop off' your dance card and that's okay. People who aren't virtuous will no longer align with you and the Universe will remove them. You will become your highest potential and your life will no longer be 'ordinary' but 'extraordinary'. You will become the next best magnificent version of yourself and you will know it, feel it, and be it, mind, body, and soul.

Seven virtues for your mind to enhance your Creativity

When you boost the seven virtues of your mind you will increase your creative ability to form and produce while gaining control over your ego-mind. You will become more innovative, original, visionary, and gifted. You may be questioning how this is all going to happen by simply focusing on and saying a few new things but that is precisely how it happens. The only way you 'become' anything or 'generate' anything is by choosing it, making up your mind, committing with your heart, and commanding with your soul. I have counselled/coached many people who have a full range of 'mental tools' and knowledge that they are using accurately to manifest and control their lives. They have read the books, listened to the tapes, and done enough therapy to go out and conquer the world but it is not happening for them. Two pieces are missing from a three-piece puzzle. They think it, but they do not 'feel' it. It cannot be found in their heart and does not come from their soul. It all sits in their head and there is a great 'disconnect'. No matter what you 'tell' yourself, if you do not 'feel' it, it is never going to happen. This is why my mantra calls to your mind, body, and soul. 'I am creative', speaks to your mind. 'I am courageous', speaks to your heart. 'I am confident', speaks to your soul.

Holifest will make more sense as we go along, but for now, you will have to trust me when I say that I am building you up and preparing you for success and abundance, starting with building on and strengthening the following seven virtues:

1 Imagination

Before you can bolster your imagination through wonder, intrigue, and close observation, you need to open up the 'space' to do it, clear your mind, and make the time. Allocate a few moments every day to be by yourself and begin to look at the world through the eyes of your 'fun loving inner-Child'. Locate the seven year old 'you' that still influences your personality and resides in your identity. The part of you that never grows up, nor would you want it to, loves spontaneity, does not want to be told it is not possible, and believes in fairy tales, make believe, and all that exists in the unseen world. The part of you that likes to go crazy, race cars, throw food, eat ice-cream, collect seashells, dress up, tell exaggerated stories, and play all day long. See the magic, be the magic. Close your eyes and create the life you want in your mind's eye. Colour it in, amp it up, shoot for the stars. There is nothing you cannot be in your imagination. There are no limits, no bounds, and no ideas too large or too small. Explore the mental landscape of your imagination and let the show begin with your wildest dreams. Create new worlds, hang some stars, and paint the moon. Rule your mental Universe and wear your crown. See yourself flying like Peter Pan or Tinkerbelle and swimming through the ocean like a dolphin. Run barefoot through fields of yellow daisies and climb trees that take you above the clouds. Feel the melting snow on your fingertips and undress in the warmth of the sun. Imagine your life, the freedom, the marvellous adventures, and escape into it as often as possible. Give yourself these moments to close your eyes and conceptualise your life. It is not a 'silly' thing to do; it is a 'compulsory' thing to do if you want to increase your creative force.

Sketching it out in your imagination is a powerful form of creation. Studies reveal that after three days, people retain only 10% of the verbal information they have received whereas they remember 65% of the drawings they have seen. The Universe is the same. Illustrate what you want in your imagination and the Universe will respond more accurately than when you speak or write about it. Fantasise it, invent it, and then 'spark' it in your mind. Draw some pencil roughs and design some thumbnails on the art board of your mind for your design agency – Universe & Co to proceed from. When you add the tremendous power of your heart and soul, so then it will be. Do not be afraid to create yourself being more than you hope for and more than you dare to dream. It is always best to think big and then go even bigger. Your own imagination is a place where you will not be judged, knocked down, or criticised. If you cannot summon the courage to imagine it the way you want it to be, it will not happen. With every challenge, doubt, or fear that comes along, simply imagine what the opposite of that would look like and escape into it for even a second. The Universe will take note and everything will begin to shuffle, move, and spin around until the result your heart desires comes into view. If something shows up in your life that you just cannot deal with or do not hold the answer to, simply imagine yourself being happy, peaceful, relaxed, and calm. Take yourself on an imaginative journey and 'escape' your current situation for something better in the 'immediate'. You can transport yourself to wherever you want by simply closing your eyes and imagining it into being.

I am imaginative

2 Strength

You will strengthen your mind and break some destructive habits by bringing awareness to your patterns of negative thinking. No matter how buoyant you are there will be times when you just cannot stay afloat. Consciousness is being able to recognise and 'catch' yourself when negative thinking takes its hold on you. You will not recognise it when you are 'in it', you will see it when you take your mind 'above it' and step into consciousness. The ego thrives on holding you captive and forcing you to believe you are your personality and your identity. Although your identity and your ego play out through you, similar to an actor playing out a script, it is not 'you'. Your ego attaches you to your identity and you 'believe' it is you until you pull back and move up in your mind to become your 'higher-self'. This is the part of you that observes the smaller 'ego you' from a different platform in your consciousness. The next time you have a negative thought, stop yourself immediately and look straight at it. What was the thought you just had? What was it about? Does it have merit? The part of your mind that you use to consciously carry out this 'cross-examination' is your higher-self, your consciousness, your awareness, and your enlightened self. The more you meet up with this part of yourself, the more you become 'enlightened' and the less 'hold' your ego and your negativity will have on you.

There are four main types of negative thinking:

(1) All or nothing thinking –

"I have to do things perfectly or not at all". "Anything short of one hundred percent is not good enough". "I have broken my diet so I might as well devour the entire fridge".

(2) Disqualifying the positives –

"Nothing went well this week". "My life is an absolute mess". "There is nothing attractive or appealing about me". "I totally suck at everything I do".

(3) Negative self-labelling –

"I am a failure". "I am hopeless". "I am not smart enough to do that". "I am just – a house-wife, just a mother, or just this or just that".

(4) Catastrophising –

"My life always goes wrong". "It is going to be a total disaster". "It always turns out bad". "He or she hates me". "I'll end up with absolutely nothing".

If any of these patterns sound familiar to you, it is time to strengthen your mind and change your thinking. Unless you are psychic, you cannot read people's minds so do not assume they do not like you. Wherever possible, avoid using the word 'should' as in 'I should do this and you should do that'. Change 'should' to 'could' or 'would' so that you don't become a 'should've' person. Do not look for approval from others. Do not disqualify the present for the future. Do not dwell on pain and do not drown in pessimism. Negative thinking is a fast track way to becoming a 'victim'. Psychological victims are weak and tragic. You do not want to go there. They get kicked down and stay down, blaming other people for how their life turned out. The pay off for victims is that they do not have to try. They remain helpless and refuse to take responsibility for their position and the circumstances they find themselves in. Strong people have authority over themselves and educate themselves in order to become more powerful and autonomous. They are self-governing and refuse to be controlled or manipulated by others. Keep your mind active and research your choices. Seek knowledge and understanding. Command yourself to stay aware of your thoughts. Remain as positive as possible and make it your goal to reach higher consciousness and develop more mental strength.

I am strong

3 Acceptance

Inner peace and calm comes through accepting 'what is'. Many people resist their current circumstances or moan about them to whoever will listen, which of course attracts more of the same. It is natural to want to complain and protest when things aren't as you would like them to be but this does not help you in the long run. Resist the urge to bitch about others, point out their flaws, and grumble about any circumstance or event that has taken place in your life. You will find that the urge passes quite quickly when you are self-disciplined and in hindsight, you will be pleased that you did not perpetuate it and draw more attention to it. I can think of at least ten things right now that I could object to, oppose, and fret to you about but I know that would not help me to Holifest, it would do the opposite and ensure that I had more things to disapprove of and moan about tomorrow. If something big is bothering you, allow yourself three minutes (actually time it) to get as angry, offended, and out-of-joint as you like. Go over the details, fell infuriated and exasperated with those involved, curse and squeal like a boiling kettle and then simmer down, cool off, let it go, accept what is, and get busy 'doing' something. If you pray for and ripen your virtues, nothing will ever turn out 'bad' for you. Eventually, everything will be okay and you will be okay. Tell yourself that this too will pass and you will be in completely different circumstances three years from now, or one year, or six months, or two weeks, or one hour – everything changes and nothing stays the same. Lao Tzu says *"Life is a series of natural and spontaneous changes.* ***Do not resist them***; *that only creates sorrow. Let reality be* *reality. Let things flow naturally forward in whatever way they like"*. It is true that what you 'resist' 'persists'. The resistance carries its own special magnetism that attracts more of the same to you and even builds and doubles. If you resist, protest, and scream out the F-word when you get a flat tyre, chances are that next time, you will break down on the Harbour Bridge with two flat tyres at the same time in the middle of peak hour traffic and things will be a whole lot worse. Accept the flat tyre, calmly change it, and carry on having increased the virtue of 'acceptance'.

* You will think I am kidding you but … I actually got a flat tyre two hours after writing the above paragraph (hungry is the soul for testing the ego) and the only thing I could think of was how lucky I was that my friend drove past and gave me a lift home to my other car so that I could pick up my son from school. I was totally 'accepting' and 'grateful' because it could have been so much worse. There are no taxi or bus services to my house so getting a lift home is a big deal. It did not occur to me until chatting in the car with my friend that I had just been writing about getting a flat tyre. The Universe has a facetious sense of humour and timing is impeccable. I later returned to the car and received help from my son who drove past on his way home from work along with a neighbour who rode past on his motorbike. Both stopped when they saw me digging through the boot of my car looking for a spare tyre that doesn't exist. Apparently Minis are equipped with a small compressor and operate a 'run flat' system. There is no way you can avoid inconveniences challenging you. They are a part of life and necessary for you to grow and build strength of character. What you can do is 'accept' them and if you are

really evolved, 'appreciate' them. I am not quite there yet with appreciating all of them however I am very aware of how they strengthen me and how supported I am when they happen. The next step is to control your reaction and response to them. No matter what happens, it could have been so much worse and every single time, help, synchronicity, and solutions are sent your way. The Universe never leaves you stranded for long. Pray for help and it comes. Guardian angels are real.

It is important to comply with what is present and accept what you have now; then from that mind-set, you can begin the steps to change. For example, if you want to lose weight, start by accepting the weight you are right now with a view to change it. There is no point starting any journey with bitterness or resistance. Acceptance is the starting point for change and forgiveness is essential to acceptance. If there is someone or something you have not forgiven, including yourself, I suggest you do. Forgiveness is the elixir of Holifest. Without a clean slate, it does not work. No good thing will come to you whilst you harbor anger, resentment, or regret. Everything that happens in your life is an opportunity to build character and shape your virtues. Forgive the hurt and release the past. No person or event needs to have 'power' over you now. Be careful that you do not confuse 'accepting' with 'enduring'. You do not ever have to endure bullying, mistreatment, or abuse. Part of acceptance is exercising the right to stand up to what you 'will not' accept from other people. Acceptance is for the things you cannot change, the past you cannot undo, and the compromises or poor decisions you have already made. What has happened has happened, let go, peacefully accept it and dismiss it from your mind. Remember my friend Jayne's mantra for the virtue of 'acceptance'? It goes like this – *'This is where I'm at and I'm accepting of that'*. It rhymes and it is fun to say. Create your own little mantras to suit whatever you are struggling with right now and find the acceptance you need to begin designing your next best step.

I am accepting

4 Compassion

Compassion toward yourself and others is the key that unlocks your creativity and corroborates your entry into the universal library of astonishing ideas where all possible concepts wait for inspiration to snatch them up and transform them into reality. Pay attention to how other people struggle and resort to bad behaviour in the hope that it will get them to where they want to go. Many people are ignorant and common sense is not that common. Other people need your compassion and acceptance. You know that you are not perfect and you probably judge yourself harshly at times. Most people are meaner to themselves than they would ever dare to be to somebody else. Brutally judging yourself or others will activate your Inner-Critic to crush your creative spirit and shame your concepts and ideas. Be kind to yourself and considerate by nature and purpose. Wherever possible, be friendly and loving. Exercise generosity without being 'too' giving. You do not want to encourage the 'taker' in another person who will then take advantage of you and milk your generosity. Do not be foolish with your money, but donate when you can. Never, and did

I say 'NEVER' be stingy or tight with money. Most people hold on to money with a vice like grip through fear of – 'there is not enough for me'. This belief is limiting and will only become a self-fulfilling prophecy. If you hold too firm, the Universe takes it off you until you learn to surrender. Be prepared to submit everything you have because you know it is all an illusion. Generosity is rewarded and what you give out comes back to you times one hundred. Offer to be of service and move gently through your life and your social circles. Look for opportunities to help others and do so with kindness and compassion.

When you take part in teamwork, encourage co-operation, create unity, and promote harmony. It is important to understand that everybody is here on earth to grow, learn, and hopefully have a tremendous amount of fun. Do not forget the fun – be fun, create fun, and chase the fun around in circles the same way my boxer pup does crazy circles on our lawn at full speed. Remember that some people are more 'evolved' and 'aware' than others and those who are younger in spirit need your tenderness and guidance. Ignorance is not bliss. It is a burden and now that you know how virtuous you are, I can safely say that you are not ignorant. You now know that building your character and firmly establishing your virtues makes you more powerful and elevates you to a position of leadership and responsibility. Virtuous people are trailblazers who light the way for those who cannot see why things do not work out and blindly believe that life is hard and cruel. People will constantly fall short of your expectations and can often let you down so do your best to not rely on others and instead be independent and self-sufficient. As often as possible, give other people a hand up and never forget those who gave you a leg up when you needed it. I make a point of remembering every kind deed, gesture, and door opening I have ever received and I am forever grateful to the people who have helped me. Lead with understanding toward those who follow your example and when they stumble, fall, or fail you, shower them with empathy, forgiveness, and compassion.

I am compassionate

5 Motivation

Did you know that you have power and 'choice' over how you distribute your mental energy? De-motivation guzzles your mental energy like a Bugatti Veyron and the virtue of motivation is your own private petrol bowser. Your mind has a certain amount of energy to distribute every day. Negative thoughts use up far more energy than positive thoughts. Now that you know you can consciously distribute your energy on a daily basis, ask yourself how you intend to use it. What will you allow yourself to think about? You use up more energy when you move out of the 'immediate' into the past or onto the future. Keeping your mind in the immediate conserves your mental consumption. Driving your mind forward into the future 'what ifs' uses a huge amount of mental fuel. Reversing back to the past 'whys' does the same. Motivation is maintained by 'parking' your mind in the immediate and dealing with the here and now. Regardless of your mental energy levels, it is impossible to remain constantly motivated. There will be times when you let yourself off the hook, times when it all feels too hard, and you just couldn't be bothered. Like the balance of everything in life, there will be times when you can readily jump through hoops and other times when you can barely drag yourself out of bed. This is 'common' and it fits in with the fluctuating cycles of life, energy, and rhythm. Allow the slump and then focus your mind on completing one task to fire up your motivation. The satisfaction of achievement will kick start your motivation and generate more of the same.

Sometimes you have to forcibly subpoena your enthusiasm and passion. There are times when it hides out, like a runaway teenager, sulking and refusing to be found and other times when you have an inner-Drill Sergeant barking orders and revving you up like a high performance sports car. There will be some occasions when a beached whale hijacks your motivation and rolls it out on the sand but you know yourself well and you know when you genuinely need to rest and recoup. Give in to yourself when you are sincerely tired or burnt out. But if you are just making excuses then you need a good crop on the neck and a stern talking to. Be stronger than your strongest excuse. Do not give that whale too much time in your head. They are beautiful mammals but you are not supposed to look or act like one. I must confess, some days my treadmill looks like a torture machine and the thought of getting on it is like pulling teeth. I am addicted to endorphins so after three days of not running I can be found grumbling around the house like a thunderstorm brewing. I always feel better knowing that I have motivated myself to exercise and released my happy peptides, lowered my stress levels, and enhanced my immune system. When I find myself struggling at the thought of running, I simply say to myself 'I am motivated' and go about putting my runners on without allowing another thought to come through my mind's door. It works like magic. Twenty minutes into my run this morning, I was feeling sluggish so I said out loud 'I am motivated'. I said it every minute for the remaining twenty minutes of my run and that last twenty minutes went so much faster and was so much easier than the first. I even increased the speed and upped the incline. I 'became' motivation. Get moving with what you want and as often as possible preserve mental fuel by living in the immediate and demanding your motivation to keep you focused on your goals.

I am motivated

6 Detachment

Being 'detached' does not mean that you have to detach from everything. To accurately understand detachment you have to look at what you actually need to 'detach' from. Buddhists 'detach' from craving and suffering. They do not detach from other people, emotions, joy, or life connection. Attachment in the negative sense happens when you get stuck or caught in habits that you have no control over or when you get caught up in materialism, negativity, destructive emotional cycles, compulsions, or addictions associated with past or present pain or trauma. In the western world, we have very little choice other than to succumb to addictions. Although not all addictions are necessarily 'harmful', all of them in some way keep you

17

disconnected from your spirituality and disrupt your inner peace. Our culture encourages and even requires you to have addictions to be able to cope with the stresses and pressures of life. Most people cannot get through the day without caffeine, sugar, obsessively connecting with technological devices or slaving at the office. I tried to kid myself into thinking that I did not have any addictions until I started to understand what they really are. Without stillness, there is no spiritual life. Doing nothing makes people anxious and being over busy causes stress.

If you lose the necessary balance of mind, body, and spirit, you will fall victim to addictive substances and processes or spiral into 'dis-ease'. There are many different types of addictions. Two main types are 'process addictions' and 'substance addictions'. Process addictions include – work, sex, excessive TV watching, gambling, shopping, spending, exercise, religion, negative thinking, and love addicted relationships. Most people are love addicted – in love with being in love, and choose another person as their 'drug of choice'. I was love addicted until the person I was unknowingly addicted to was taken away resulting in a tremendous amount of emotional pain. I then had to do some serious work on my self-esteem before entering into another relationship. Overcoming love addiction can be harder than quitting drugs, alcohol, or any other serious addiction because of the 'emotional' attachment involved. Our pop music reinforces our love addiction with lyrics that go something like – 'I can't live without you in my life', or 'I can't survive without you', or 'you are my everything, without you I'm nothing'. There is even a song by Avicci titled 'Addicted to you'. Love addiction is very common and most people do not realise the hold it has over them until they 'break up' with that 'addiction'. Substance addictions include – food (especially processed foods high in sugar and fat), coffee, alcohol, prescription drugs, hard drugs, and smoking. There are also different levels of addiction with a 'level four' addiction requiring professional help and rehabilitation. The memories and past experiences that cause you pain are the calamitous patterns that ensure you become 'hooked' on substances, processes, or behaviours that sabotage your creativity and block your spiritual ability to channel pure creativity.

Live in the 'immediate' and become aware of everything in and around you in order to create more intimacy, more connection and more relatedness with other people and with life. Detachment is the older sibling of 'Surrender'. Surrender is 'letting go' of control. Detachment does not need control in the first place. Surrender develops your faith in the flow of life and connects you with your higher-self. What you 'can' control is within you and what you cannot control is everything else on the outside. When you fully understand this reality, you can start to focus and work on what you can control and then you will become empowered. It is a relief to break the illusion that you need to control everything. The need to control comes from fear. Connect with other people by teaching them, mentoring them, educating them, and providing personal assistance to them. Giving your time away is much more valuable than writing a cheque or handing out money. It is sometimes hard to give away money but always much harder to give away time. Time is far more precious because it can never be replaced. Engage in an altruistic endeavour. Look into charities, world issues, community support programs, caring for the elderly or the homeless. The more you give of yourself, and are of service to others, the more serene and happy you become. This has been proven many times over through experience and through psychological studies. Let go of the things that no longer serve you and give up the things that harm you with decided detachment. Liberate yourself from the need to control everything and everyone around you and 're-assign' your inner-Control Freak from the war mission of 'got to control' to the new peace and relief mission of 'got to detach'.

I am detached

7 Patience

Patience is a virtue that conjoins with tolerance. These two go hand in hand and many people lack both or have very little of one or the other. Things will come up in your life that you determine to be 'intolerable', annoying, and outright frustrating. Expanding your patience and accepting these things is valuable to your creativity. Ideas and solutions do not always come fast so it helps to be able to wait it out with patience and faith. Creativity is strangled by stress and agitation. I had a graphic design contract in a studio that was a bit like a sweatshop. The clients were demanding and the creative team were only just functioning in survival mode. There was an expectation that artwork of the highest standard should be 'churned out' regardless of the stressful, hurried environment. I was handed a brief to create a poster and told that it needed to be completed in the next fifteen minutes. My mind went blank like a sheer white canvas. I had nothing, not even a dot on the page. I felt my heart race and my face flush. My creativity was stifled and murdered right behind my eyes. There was no patience and no space to open up and receive the flow of good ideas. Creativity dries up under pressure. Have you noticed that your best ideas come when you are showering, daydreaming, or driving? This is because your DMN – default mode network, a network of interacting brain regions become active when you are not focused on the outside world and your mind is wakefully resting and only semi-engaged in what you are doing. When your subconscious mind takes over and carries out tasks for you, free space is created in your mind and ideas bubble to the surface; your attention is turned inwards and you are able to make insightful connections. Being sleepy or lightly drunk also allows for creativity. We all know that highly creative people often turn to drugs and alcohol. I am not suggesting that; but I do love a glass of red or two, okay – sometimes three, and I often find a fabulous idea waiting excitedly at the bottom of the bottle. Bright ideas come forward when you exercise, listen to music, and shower because of the dopamine that is released in your brain through these relaxing, distracting, pleasurable experiences.

Creativity, ideas, and concepts require 'space' and the same applies to creating a life worth living. Without time for yourself and the space to 'turn off' your chattering mind, inspiration is unobtainable. Meditation is the training ground for patience. Your ego-mind likes to be occupied. Robin Sharma said *"The mind is a wonderful servant, but a terrible master"*. Yoga is a useful practise for demanding your attention back to the immediate through physical, energy centred poses. Stillness is a state that requires practise. Bruce MacLelland said *"the wisest men, those who could see the farthest into any project, were **quiet, calm** men, who could not be easily disturbed"*. Before you can begin meditation, you need to push through the conflict that comes from preferring to be someplace else and the pull to be doing something else. Creative forces cannot flow through you when you live in a perpetual struggle to just 'be' and allow your mind to swing from branch to branch like a crazy monkey. You cannot force it. Brilliance does not materialise when you are under the pump. Channelling creativity only happens when you are present, in the immediate, and open to receive. Brilliance does not answer to the clock or adhere to timelines or unrealistic client demands. Brilliance requires a spacious desk in your mind, situated in a quiet corner with room to stretch its legs and wait patiently for its mystical muse. Creative brilliance thrives on patience and reaches you through the rhythm of your breath. When you start your next creation, make sure you begin with perseverance, open your gifts in the middle, and then end with patience.

I am patient

Seven virtues for your body to enhance your Courage

Establishing the seven virtues of your body will sustain your physical being and increase your courage while building strength and stamina. Without courage, you will move through life being submissive and answering to fear and doubt. Fear is a lowly ruler and a lousy advisor. Although a certain amount of healthy fear is required for your survival, you have been wired to expect the worst. Unfastening those wires and calming your heart is vital to Holifest. Nothing happens until you feel it happening in your heart, in your body, in your humanness. If your mind is not aligned with your heart, whatever you want or deserve is not going to come to you. Your body is where 'deserving' is initiated and located. Your stomach is the home of your self-esteem and self-worth. When your self-esteem takes a 'hit' and somebody puts you down, you may describe it as a 'kick in the guts'. Often people overeat and put on weight to 'protect' their vulnerability and 'hide out'. This weight transfers to the stomach area. When you do something wrong and feel bad or ashamed you might feel 'sick to the stomach'. When somebody hurts you, you could feel 'crushed', 'broken hearted', or 'ripped apart'. These are all physical descriptions because this is where it hurts the most. Your emotional body is located in your stomach and in your heart. Looking after your body is crucial to Holifest. The best way to bolster your self-esteem on the physical level is to train your abdominal muscles and strengthen them with static contractions, sit-ups, or crunches. If you are strong in your body, you will be equally strong in your life.

You must honour your flesh, maintain your wellness, and vibrate your physical self at the highest possible frequency, starting with building on and strengthening the following seven virtues:

1 Commitment

Being able to commit to someone or something takes stamina and often endurance. Muhammad Ali said *"Champions aren't made in gyms. Champions are made from something they have **deep inside them** ... a desire, a dream, a vision. They have to have last-minute stamina, they have to be a little faster, and they have to have the skill and the will. **But the will must be stronger than the skill"**.* Perseverance trumps talent. Talent without drive is useless. It is like skill without will. I know many talented people but they aren't where they want to be because they need to have a fire lit under them. So many people dream of being at the top but they aren't prepared to put in the work and effort that is required to be better than the rest. They want to become elite without sacrifice, pain, or any level of discomfort. Whatever it is that you want to achieve, expect a marathon because nothing comes easy. Having dreams that you are not willing to back with power and force is like having a Ferrari parked in the garage with the engine pulled out. Muhammad Ali said ***"the will must be stronger than the skill"***. He was right. Cleverness and expertise alone is as useless as a sail without wind. Your ability to commit, stay loyal, and purposeful is your 'wind'.

Finding 'last-minute stamina' is what sets you apart and makes you a champion. It is the ability to 'dig deep', persist, and insist when the going gets tough, things go wrong, and other people say you can't. The power for stamina is generated by your heart and fed by your spirit. Your will to survive is also sustained by your spirit. Your spirit lives in your mind, body, and soul. Your heart is like the engine for your Ferrari. Very few people make it to the top of their chosen field and very few people reach their goals or realise their dreams. The reason for this is lack of persistence and the inability to fully 'commit' to what is required of them. Achievement may ask you to forfeit, endure, and at times forgo what other people are enjoying or indulging in. You may have to 'miss out' on the fun and bunker down to get to where you are headed. You may have to renounce and waive but if it is really that important to you, you will do it willingly; knowing that the end result is worth it. Bruce MacLelland said ***"know thyself is the deepest and best advice ever given to mankind.*** *It embraces the knowledge that* ***character or self can be strengthened and ennobled;*** *that force can be added to one; that the mind attracts success in all things as it is freed from jealousy, envy, distrust, ill will, anger, haste, and fear"*. Commit to knowing yourself fully before determining your ultimate success; and then set about strengthening your character. Carl Jung said *"your vision will become clear only when you **look into your heart** ... Who looks outside dreams. Who looks inside, awakens"*. Now is your time to awaken, define what you really want, and firmly commit to achieving and acquiring it.

I am committed

2 Ethical

These days, there are more hoaxes going around than you can shake a stick at. Some are totally obvious whereas others are quite sophisticated and hard to identify. I fell victim to one from a pretend 'tax office'. It was with regard to a tax refund nominating an amount that I was actually due to receive. I still wonder how they could have known the exact amount but that is the risk with the internet. These 'scammers' asked for an account number to deposit the money into. I mindlessly filled out the form and viola, scam! My anticipated tax return nearly wound up costing me money. I often cringe when I imagine the innocent, the elderly, the unsuspecting people who also fall victim to these unethical people. Psychologist Dr Phil McGraw refers to unethical people as 'BAITERs'. 'BAITER' is abbreviated from – *backstabbers, abusers, imposters, takers, exploiters, and reckless*. BAITERs have an air of arrogant entitlement that gives them away. Some BAITERs believe that whatever you have is theirs. This includes your money, your house, your reputation, your client, your share, your job, your partner, your dog, etc., and they have no guilt when they make a move on any of these things. If you are paying attention, they will show you these patterns early on in your relationship. They also have a history of short-term relationships. BAITERs will brag about out-smarting people or ripping them off.

BAITERs are haters by another name, and more clearly defined. Bruce MacLelland said *"it was observed that haters' bodies were always tensely drawn, the muscles incapable of relaxation, both mind and body shriveled and contracted, functions deranged and the bodies full of aches and pains. The explanation was that hatred; jealousy and despondency had an attraction for a tense, inharmonious frame of mind and produced the corresponding effects in the body"*. Your body and your health are directly effected and influenced by the quality of your character and behaviour. Unethical people have no empathy for others. They are self-serving and have a sense of 'privilege' whereby they feel that the world owes them something and they are determined to 'take it'. They are tight with money and miserly. They do whatever it takes to make sure they get ahead with no regard for you. Living a life of fairness, righteousness, and decency is what makes you honest and legitimate. Raising the bar for your ethics, values, and morals is imperative to shaping your heart and body to Holifest. Acting with integrity and increasing your goodness will give you more veracity to Holifest your way to success and prosperity while building character at the same time with the virtue of ethics.

I am ethical

3 Excellence

There is already excellence in you and you will bring this forth when you have the courage to be your authentic self. Excellence of character requires originality and authenticity. What holds you back from showing up in the world as the 'real' you? What masks have you been wearing in order to be accepted, liked, and admired? Have you hidden your genuine self to gain approval from others? Have you acted with honour and without fail honoured yourself? These are all big questions that deserve some reflection. No matter what you are called to do, respond with excellence. Bring your authenticity and greatness to every area of your life. Charles Dickens said *"My meaning simply is, that whatever I have tried to do in life, I have tried with all my heart to do well; that whatever I have devoted myself to, I have devoted myself to completely; that in great aims and in small, I have always been thoroughly in earnest"*. Be in earnest, diligent, and fervent with every chore, task, and job you commence, even the easy, tiny, quick, and simple ones. I used to think that I had to do something big and famous in order to matter in this world but the truth is, it doesn't matter what you do, it matters what you become while you are doing what you do. When you come to do your next task or job, do it well; do it to the best of your ability, and do it with excellence. Your contribution to this world is no less important than the next person. Many people have a bad habit of 'comparing up' and feeling 'less than'. You never need to feel inadequate. Nobody has the 'perfect' life and everything good carries a shadow. Do not ever wish to be somebody else or have what somebody else has. If it were meant to be yours, it would be. Instead, compare yourself with 'excellence' and start from there.

I am surprised by how many people fall into the habit of answering "How are you"? with "Not bad", or "Alright", "Ok", or my absolute least favourite answer –"I'm so tired". If you say you are tired, you are affirming that you are tired and you will continue to 'be' tired. 'I am' statements are powerful and self-fulfilling. They are an announcement, an affirmation, and an attestation to where you are positioned and how you claim to be in that very moment and in your life in general. Even if you are feeling like crap, or less than peppy, remember your virtues and remind yourself about the power of 'I am' statements. When someone next asks you how you are, instead of saying "Not too bad", or "Reasonable", try saying "I am excellent" and mean it. On average, I am asked how I am roughly five to ten times per day which provides quite a few opportunities for me to mentally and verbally affirm how I am or how I would really like to be. It is an interesting 'experiment' to observe how other people answer – "How are you"? Pay attention to how people describe themselves to be and it will re-enforce for you how important this simple custom really is. Notice what they say, how they say it, their body language, and their energy. I guarantee that you will never say "I am not bad" ever again once you observe how 'un-excellent' it is. Some people who ask you how you are, do not give much of a flying 'you know what' how you really are, it is just a formality. You could answer "I am up the creek without a paddle" and they would probably respond "that's great, now let's talk about me". When you next ask somebody how he or she is going, be authentic, and make a 'genuine' enquiry. Be sure that every interaction you have with others is legitimate, bona fide, and cloaked in excellence.

I am excellent

4 Faith

Do you take risks? Are you able to operate outside of your comfort zone or has it become a comfort 'dot'? Do you settle for less than you wish for? Are you flexible with outcomes or do you feel disappointed if things do not work out exactly the way you planned? Opening your faith is like peeling the skin off your heart and exposing the flesh – pure, vulnerable, and raw. It takes great courage to run the gauntlet with faith in your heart. It requires trust, hope, and optimism. Faith is what lets you take responsibility for yourself and for your life. Growing faith in yourself is one thing but investing your faith in the Supreme Intelligence is another. This usually happens through one or two avenues – pain or intense pain. I have had moments in my life when I felt entirely alone, abandoned, deserted. I was in a place of misery where no one could co-exist with me. I did not want or expect anyone else to sit it out with me. It was my cross to bear and bear it I did. But I was not alone. There was an unknown force, a subtle presence that helped me carry that cross. A 'force' that sat on the end of my bed when I slept alone, that hovered at my window while I stared out in hopelessness. Before long, I connected deeply with this mystical force of energy and my soul revived on the pure love it emanated. I was raised Catholic and attended church as a child but my church now is a secluded rock set deep in the Australian bush. Like many people, I imagined 'God' to be a man in the sky with a grey beard, wearing a large robe, surrounded by pretty angels. I believed this God was an authoritarian 'parent' who would punish me if I did the wrong thing or committed a 'sin'. Everything changed when I read Neale Donald Walsch's book 'Conversations with God'. My whole perception shifted and thankfully the man in the sky faded away. God became something much larger, more powerful, almighty, indescribable, and visually impossible to imagine. I call this God 'Supreme Intelligence'. You are free to call your God whatever name pleases you. When I look for God now, I see a white light, pure love, ultimate intelligence, divinity, and holiness. I found this Supreme Intelligence at the centre of pain and this ultimate force has never left my mind, heart, or soul. It resides in me and issued me a faith that is tireless, endless, and unwavering. When I was a child, I often prayed, and my prayers began with "Dear God …" as I imagined him sitting on a cloud, looking down at me. To do this now feels like the 'little me' talking to God, or even begging. I now find myself simply opening my soul to the ultimate power and finding a 'connection' to the centre of myself. This does not happen through my mind, this happens through my faith. When you feel hurt, alone, lost, confused, or afraid, close your eyes and say the prayer "I need and ask for help with …" Believe that something hears you and expect a miracle. You have put into play a change, a shift, and a transformation. It is coming and it is changing. Just have faith.

I am faithful

5 Justice

Much of what happens in life does not appear to be fair and it probably isn't. Bad things happen to good people. People lie, cheat, and steal. Children suffer. Many get hurt. Murderers walk free and innocents go to jail. The human justice system is flawed, often corrupt, and rarely ever affordable or reliable. From the outside looking in, it often appears that it pays to be a criminal. They seem to get the long end of the stick. It is generally up to the poor victim to prove that they are actually a victim at their own expense and distress. Many people give up before they even begin because what they are chasing usually works out to be less than what it will cost to chase it. If this system were all we had to rely on, it would be a very depressing realisation. Justice is served at three levels – the ego seeks justice through developing counter attacks, the heart seeks justice through developing resilience, and the soul seeks justice through developing wisdom. It is understandable that you would like to see justice served and it is reasonable to wish for revenge when somebody hurts you or takes what is rightfully yours. Plotting your next counterblow only annihilates your inner-peace. Justice is best served when you build the virtue of resilience in your heart and expand the virtue of wisdom through your soul. You will know you have reached a high level of self-actualisation when you can move toward being grateful for the unjust things that happen to you. Not grateful for the pain of the actual event, trauma, or loss, but grateful for the growth and strength of character you developed through surviving it, the resilience you developed through bearing the pain, and the acceptance you reached through surrendering the need to control your fate and focusing instead on the quality of your destiny.

If you look up the 'List of ongoing armed conflicts' in the world, you will find it to be a very sobering web page. We are not good at dealing with 'conflict' and we are willing to sacrifice lives in order to get what we want. I couldn't even guess as to when humans are going to evolve beyond this, perhaps never. You can however choose to evolve beyond it in yourself and put an end to any internal or external conflict you may have by commanding peace with your past. I came to realise that the path to inner peace is found through relinquishing the need for external justice and calming the ego. Do you believe in karma? Karma is a Sanskrit term that means 'action' or 'doing'. In the Buddhist tradition, karma refers to 'intentional action' and it is considered that the intentions of a person determine what kind of rebirth will take place in the cycle of life, death, and rebirth. Karma works on the principle of 'cause' and 'effect' whereby the intent and actions of an individual influence the future of that individual. Often we do not see karma work its magic. Some people appear to 'get away with' being cruel, self-serving, and even outright evil. I have noticed that moviemakers and storytellers always portray the 'good guy' coming out on top. This is because the viewers demand justice. Our craving for justice would never let the villain win. I have a jury that sits in my heart and demands truth. I live by my truth as it is whispered to me through my intuition and guidance is sent from the Supreme Intelligence. You cannot control the outside world, you can only control your inside world. Let your heart be your courtroom and in this courtroom, you will always find justice. Judge yourself kindly and fairly. Observe others to discern for yourself whether or not their behaviour is appropriate so that you can then determine how to behave yourself. Give up the need to judge and condemn them. This only amplifies their influence in the world. Trust in the Universal System of Justice to do what we are powerless to do. Let love be the judge and while accepting that evil exists, do not ever submit to it. Evil exists in your unconscious mind and in the collective unconscious in order for consciousness to exist and for you to have a conscience in your mind, heart, and soul. Without evil there would be no consciousness in the same way that dark would not exist without light. Existence requires polarity, opposition, and division so that you have the 'choice' and 'opportunity' to exercise your will, to strengthen your heart, and to satisfy your soul. Simply choose higher consciousness in yourself and use the evil that you hear about and experience in the world to repel the primeval darkness in your psyche and move you closer to the light that shines from your soul. Develop your ability to be sympathetic, compassionate, and empathetic, and above all, be fair and just with everyone including yourself.

I am just

6 Resilience

Trauma and Tragedy are the grandparents of Resilience. Mr and Mrs Pain are the parents. Mrs Pain gave birth through adversity, hardship, and suffering. Resilience was born. Your resilience can be recognised by how quickly and easily you 'bounce back' or 'get up and dust off' after a serious setback or disappointment. Research has shown that resilience is actually 'ordinary' rather than 'extraordinary'. Resilience is commonly demonstrated. It is naturally within the human spirit to be resilient. It is not rare but it can be further developed. As a counsellor/coach, I have heard many stories and been privy to a great deal of pain, anguish, and hardship. I am continually in awe of how amazingly buoyant, and resilient people are. The reason I love Positive Psychology is that it studies what is 'right' with people rather than what is 'wrong' with them as traditional psychology has always done. Positive Psychology refers to 'post-traumatic growth' as opposed to 'post-traumatic stress' (PTSD). Many people grow and develop strength of character after the loss of a loved one, a relationship, a serious health problem, or a workplace or financial disaster. I have counselled/coached many people who have lost partners, children, suffered tremendous adversity, and fought back with tenacity, stamina, and endurance. Although these people would give anything to have the people back they have lost or change the circumstances of their challenge, trauma, or struggle, not one person has ever said that they would like to go back to being the person they were before the tragedy. Their losses have made them even stronger than they were before. They have grown, become more resilient, stepped into aggrandizement, become more courageous, and experienced an awe-inspiring transformation. Transformation is the jewel that emerges from the centre of resilience. It is the reward that insists upon your growth, the spreading of your wings, and the certainty of your ability to take flight in your life.

The road to resilience is a steep goat track that requires behaviours, thoughts, and actions that are conducive to healing and processing grief. Resilience increases your self-reliance and self-dependability. When push comes to shove, the only person who truly has your back, who you can fully rely on, is 'you'. Building character requires you to develop a strong sense of self-trust. The passage through grief is painfully lonely and the itinerary includes activities such as – shock, denial, anger, bargaining, depression, and finally acceptance and repositioning. Migrating back from grief allows you to 'move-on' and look at life again through a completely new and different lens. Grief is exhausting, unpredictable, relentless, and excruciatingly insulate. Nobody can feel it for you, process it for you, or heal it for you. It is something that you have to go through yourself and when you come out the other end, you are forever changed. I drew the analogy between grief and glass when I visited the Venetian island of Murano many years ago and watched the glass artisans heat sand to 1,700 degrees, melt it, add chemicals to produce colour, and manipulate it into the most beautiful, delicate glass figurines imaginable. Like grief, through extreme, intense circumstances, and the forceful change of materials, something beautiful, majestic, and ceremonious is created. Resilience comes through transformation. Your misfortunes and sufferings bring with them the gift of resilience and shape you into something even more superb and exquisite than you were before.

I am resilient

7 Cleanliness

To Holifest, you need order, sequence, and cleanliness. If you want to be attractive groom yourself, if you want a new roommate clean the house, if you want a new job polish your resume, if you want to win blue ribbons service your equipment, if you want a new car wash the one you have, if you want a new body exercise and eat well, if you want visitors sweep the porch, if you want a date set up a profile or buy a new outfit, if you want more clients organise your office. I am sure you get the picture and picture it is. Create the scene. This is where effort comes in. If you do not want to spend time at the doctor's surgery or in the hospital, eat well, exercise, sleep, play, dance, and stay present. You have to 'do' something to make something else happen. This is the formula to cause and effect. If you do not shake the fruit tree, the fruit stays on, and your basket remains empty. Nothing happens without some effort and Holifest is no different. Cleaning is one of the best things you can do to create flow in your life. Cleaning is also very good for processing grief because it is 'transformative' and it changes the vibration of what you are cleaning while lifting your energy and mood. If you were selling your home, you would present it in the best possible way. You would scrub the bathroom, mow the lawn, and trim the hedges. Presentation is the whole shebang along with cleanliness and personal appearance. Pride in your physical self is essential. It is good to take pride in yourself but do not confuse pride with arrogance. Feeling proud of yourself and celebrating your achievements is positive and you deserve a good pat on the back when you have done well. Holifest requires structure, systems, routines, and most importantly, happy hormones.

This is how you get those happy hormones bouncing around –

- Aerobic exercise gives you endorphins
- Music you love gives you dopamine
- Healthy carbohydrates give you serotonin
- Pleasurable activities give you oxytocin
- Stress-relieving activities balance oestrogen
- Clean eating balances progesterone

Cleaning your body and strengthening your heart and lungs is key to Holifest. Your body is happy when it is fit, toned, lean, flexible, and the perfect shape for you. If you do not have a fitness routine, now is the time to start one. Exercise needs to be scheduled and prioritised. Exercise is to your body what cleaning your teeth is to your mouth. If you over eat or use food to feed your pain, it is time to restrain and admit what is happening. Your body does not need to be 'stuffed' full of food and it is not a garbage can for all the leftovers. Many people 'mindlessly' go to the fridge or the pantry and eat out of boredom, habit, or emotional imbalance. Before you eat the very next thing, ask yourself whether or not you are actually hungry, ask if you need it, and determine if you are conscious about it. If you are having a piece of chocolate because you want it and you are allowing yourself, that's fine; but if you are gormandising the whole family block because you are upset about something or avoiding something else then that's not good. Allow space in your belly for your self-esteem to grow and expand. Leave the table satisfied, not loaded, and if you are not hungry, do not eat. I have counselled/coached many people who have the same eating 'disorder' I used to have. I call it 'All or Nothing eating'. The roller coaster of all or nothing eating looks something like this – I have been 'good' all week and eaten well and now the weekend is here. It is time to let my hair down and hoover in whatever fits through the perimeter of my very open mouth. Monday comes around and now I am back to being 'good' and if I so much as eat one tiny morsel of 'naughty' food then it's food-fest, pig-out, binge, and bulge time. My sensible eating plan goes out the window and I feel like a foie gras duck. A much better option would go something like this – I eat healthy, nourishing, natural food 80% of the time and 20% of the time I eat whatever the hell I want with no guilt and I consciously step off the mind numbing rollercoaster.

There is no such thing as 'good' food and 'bad' food so stop punishing yourself for eating a biscuit. Food is food. There are just things that you choose to eat more of because you feel good for doing so and things that you choose to eat in moderation because bingeing leaves you feeling sick and nauseous. If your naughty 'inner-Deviate' jumps out of the shadow to take you partying and you wind up in bed with a family size pizza at 4am, do not flog yourself, just get back on track tomorrow and start afresh. Guilt does not inspire Holifest. Holifest requires a clean physical, internal, and external environment. Similar to feng shui where you need to be free of clutter, breathe clean air, and have natural light for good energy to flow to you and through you. Make your body, home, and office a sanctuary. Mess and chaos leads to stress. It is important to be neat and tidy in order to flow with creative inspiration. Clutter and rubbish vibrate at a low level and block feng shui. You can freshen things up with a coat of paint or a makeover if you need to but make sure your home is the place you love to be. Clean up your desk, sort out your filing, and throw out old paperwork that you no longer need. Buy some nice desk accessories, sharpen your pencils, and replace your dead pens. Clean out your fridge, throw out expired foods, wipe down the shelves, and re-stack with food for your health. Clean out your wardrobe and throw out anything you have not worn in over two years. Be ruthless and mercilessly cull the clothes you know you will not get around to wearing again. Throw out anything that is ripped, stained, too 80's, too tight, or too young and 'try-hard'. Old world glamour, style, and class will always outdo modern, barely covered, look-at-me, and whoops-I-just-popped-out. I am no 'prude' but if you need an example on how to dress, think Princess Grace Kelly or Sean Connery dressed as James Bond. Clean out your draws, rip down the cobwebs, throw out the garbage, and free the cupboards of the hodgepodge they have become. Create a new room, corner or space, just for you where you can exercise, do yoga, reflect, visualise, and meditate.

I am clean

Seven virtues for your soul to enhance your Confidence

Evolving the seven virtues of your soul maximises your confidence and allows you to let-go and trust that there is a higher power watching out for you, looking after you, and kicking goals for you. Confidence in your mind comes from ego whereas confidence in your soul comes from knowing that you are a part of the Supreme, Divine, and Boundless Intelligence that created infinity and is the manifestation of eternity. Your soul is the part of you that is sacred, mystical, otherworldly, and connected to all that is. A strong soul emerges from strength of character and the one true power of love and strength of heart. Your soul has an intelligence that is not unlike yet way beyond the intelligence of your immune system. In other words, it knows what to do to heal you and keep you well and balanced. It defies science but it exists and operates in and through you. This 'knowing' fundamentally leads to your success. Successful people are soulful, sanguine, self-assured, and self-reliant; they are prepared to fail and often do, but they have the courage to try again and they never give up, quit, or expect somebody else to do it for them. Confidence builds when you can allow the Supreme Intelligence to control your life. Soulful-Confident people are not 'control freaks'. Increased confidence gives you the ability to aim high and know that you will eventually make the mark. Confidence is different to arrogance in that confidence is tied to humility. Arrogance on the other hand is the indigestible 'totally stuck-up' with a side order of 'high-and-mighty'. Confidence is attractive and assertive without being aggressive and 'cocky'. Soulful-Confident people do not show off. They do not have to. They have a quiet, steady assuredness that transmits from their soul and radiates out in the form of pure magnetic confidence.

Soulful-Confident people are not conceited, vain, or self-serving; instead they look to boost other people and build them up so that they have more friends to play with at the top who are also on their game, appreciating life, and giving off phenomenal vibes. Confidence that shines from a strong connected soul is by far the most attractive attribute you could ever possess. It is a confidence that outranks ego-generated confidence. People who have gained their confidence from the outside world are like hollow trees that fall over in a strong wind; whereas people who have gained their confidence from their inside world have grown strong roots that withstand forceful winds and wild storms. Soulful-Confident people stand out from the crowd. They are memorable and they know how to move people, make them think, and inspire them. Soulful-Confident people are different and original; they aim to fit-out as opposed to fit-in. Soulful-Confident people are wild, crazy, unpredictable, and refuse to conform. They are confident enough to break the rules, bold enough to live life on their own terms, and do not have to apologise for being unique, going against the grain, or skipping along the road less travelled rather than walking the path well worn. Soulful-confident people shrug their shoulders at adversity and leap before they look. They dance with the hope that everybody is watching and they march to the beat of their very own big, boisterous, deafening drum.

Soulful-Confident people refuse to fit the mould and know that comparing themselves to others would be an absurd, useless exercise. You are about to evolve your ego-confidence into soulful-confidence, starting with building on and strengthening the following seven virtues:

1 Assertiveness

Training and riding horses has helped me to understand the true meaning of assertiveness. Horses look for and respond to leadership yet they resist and recoil from aggression. They let you know when you are being too strong and if you give them something to pull against, they will pull back even harder. If you lean on them, they will lean on you and they become dull to the leg if you nag them with constant pressure and reminders. The same goes for people. I gave a talk recently on 'conflict resolution' and highlighted the fact that people are not good at listening. The reason for this is that from a young age, you learn to 'not listen'. Firstly, your parents ask you to do things that you do not want to do. I tell my son over and over to put a jumper on when he goes outside in winter. He hates wearing jumpers so he has 'learnt' to not hear me asking him. Secondly, teachers tell the class more than once what their assignment is. Teachers know that half of the children aren't listening so they repeat the assignment task four or five times. The children soon learn that they do not have to listen the first time because the instructions will inevitably be repeated and they will catch them on the third or fourth round. Every day, you are bombarded with information and advertising. You learn to tune out and block the noise, which again teaches you to stop listening.

When you communicate, take your time, and do not spurt-out the first 'reactive' thought that springs to mind. If you are formatting a response to a conflict in writing, do not run with your ego-reaction that will likely be 'volatile' or 'defensive'. Speak to your conscious mind and ask which response is required to steer you toward the 'high-road' and then register it with your heart and endorse it with your soul. You will be glad that you did not just 'jump in' and go with your initial retort. Remember also that you are dealing with people who have stopped listening. Constantly nagging and repeating instructions and requests is not being assertive. To be assertive is to be decisive and purposeful. Remaining in a state of indecision is not being conclusive and determined. Assertiveness requires confidence, underpins determination, and gives you the grit you need to get things done. Many people are indecisive and this stems from fear of making a mistake or making the wrong choice. If you are usually a competent person, making a mistake actually makes you more likeable according to social psychology and the 'pratfall effect'. People who never make mistakes are less likeable because they come across as being 'perfect', flawless, and hard to relate to. This creates distance and gives off the unachievable air of invincibility. Making mistakes rates you 'human', more empathetic, accessible, and 'real'. People who share their errors, mistakes, and mishaps are warmer and friendlier. In reality, you cannot make a mistake when decision-making; you can only make a compromise or conduct an internal negotiation. It is either this or that or a combination of both. There is no reason to hesitate when your heart and mind lead you to your next best step. If you are hesitating, it is because your guiding alignment is off. What questions are surfacing in your mind or stirring in your heart? When you think with your heart the path becomes clear and you can make a strong, resolved choice, which is being mentally assertive – powered by soul.

I am assertive

2 Determination

Years ago, I visited the small town of Siena, in Italy, and happened to walk into the church that holds the entombed body of Savina Petrilli. I picked up a little book on her life and was moved to read that when news spread following her death on April 18, 1923, many wept, especially 'the poor'. I was drawn to regard the determination that this slender, fragile woman exhibited throughout her life via her devotion to God and her commitment to the poor. At the age of ten, Savina read an account of the life of Saint Catherine of Siena and was captivated by her story and determined to follow in her footsteps. After a private audience with Pope Pius IX, Savina established a religious congregation devoted to Catherine of Siena. It was said that Savina was 'marked in some way' and that God had his 'eye on her, shaping her by his hand'. How does God shape you with his hand, so to speak? What is it that you have been cut out to do, selected for, designed and created to attend to with fierce determination? You need something in your life that gives it great meaning, something you are drawn to, called forth for that gives you a definite purpose. There is something out there that requires your gifts. What are your gifts? Gifts are not something that you use only for yourself; they are things that you share with others and things that add context to the world.

Savina was dedicated to doing God's work with conviction, and developed an ardent love for the poor. By the age of twenty-six, she had fifty-six children in her care. Savina's determination powered up her dedication, attachment, and enthusiasm for a purpose outside of herself, larger than her, that was extended to her from the Supreme Intelligence through her soul. Savina Petrilli was beatified in 1988, (the step right before sainthood). Although you may not be earmarked for sainthood, there is something out there worth powering up for and becoming determined about. Determination rises out of passion. What are you passionate about? What motivates 'devotion' in you? What is something that you are selflessly drawn to do that you would do without needing payment or compensation? I know without a doubt that my gift is 'helping people' and that comes in many forms including motherhood, speaking, and writing. When you follow your soul-determination, you do things because you would shrivel and fade if you did not. For example, I would write this book even if I knew that nobody would ever read it because my soul has asked it of me. You also have abilities and an undertaking that is exclusively for you. Your gifts emerge from your soul, speed up your heart, and engage with your mind. They feel like 'instinct'. You instinctively know that you can handle the task, answer the call, and rise to the challenge. The total purpose of your soul is to bring forth your gifts, exercise your reason for being here, and add to the overall 'creation' of the world through you. Inspire your heart and mind with some form of dedication that gives your life intensity. Your soul calls on your spirit, your life force, to make this happen. Your spirit is the energetic electricity in you that surges when you have a rush of excitement or intense joy; when you are fired-up about something and especially when you are fiercely determined.

I am determined

3 Self-discipline

Your soul commands you to structure your inner-life and shape the interior of your being through self-discipline, stillness, the practise of thought-prayer, and channelling grace. Grace flows to you through the circular process of thought-prayer. A prayer is really just a 'thought' or a 'wish' accompanied by the power of grace with an emotion attached. This is evidenced by the 'quality' of the thought. Prayer is a thought that comes into your mind, via your

47

heart, direct from your soul. The practise of prayer does not require you to be religious; it requires you to be 'soulful' and 'confident'. Prayers that are sent by you for the good of another person carry pure grace with them and like a boomerang that you hurl out into the unknown, that grace is returned to you to illuminate your soul, warm your heart, and add to your character. Prayers, like a letter, need a recipient. They need someone or something to open them and make them manifest. Remembering to pray amidst the busy life you lead is an act of self-discipline, one that yields a high return. To have grace flowing to you and through your life is the difference between walking and gliding. Grace gives you that extra dimension. Prayer, like Holifest, is a thought that carries the strength of your heart, generated by the power of your soul. You must understand that harmful thoughts directed at another person also carry power and produce a definite result. The boomerang has two sides and can be thrown both ways. It is tempting to wish for revenge on those who have hurt you, but letting go and letting grace is a far better option than having the boomerang return only to smack you in the back of the head.

People who pray and reach out to others have a special 'quality' about them. They have a wonderful pulsating energy that can be felt the minute they walk into a room. They radiate love and have a strong attracting power. Amongst the most inspirational people in the world are those who have overcome adversity and those who have gone without to help others. Whatever you do for one person, you do for everybody. According to quantum physics, every 'particle' in existence knows what every other particle it has ever interacted with is doing. This principle is known as 'Entanglement'. When a particle meets another similar particle, their energy states become entangled and no matter how far apart they are, what happens to one influences the other. This 'action at a distance' is proof that the power of prayer is 'real'. There is some sort of subatomic exchange between particles, a communication of energy going back and forth. All particles are comprised of energy. The 'Zero Point Field' equations suggest that each particle has a single field that connects all particles; all matter, everywhere, including people, and their thoughts. There is only one energy field around everything and everyone is a part of it; everyone and everything is 'entangled' within it. Imagine that everything is floating in a big bowl of jelly. When one person moves they create ripples that can be felt by everything else. You cannot think, say, or do anything that does not have an effect on everybody and everything in the Universe.

Your brain has its own electromagnetic field. All electromagnetic fields are connected through the zero point field along with the energy of everybody's thoughts. This explains the phenomenon of telepathy, where another person can pick up your thoughts from across the globe. Have you ever had the thought to ring somebody and suddenly they ring you? Have you thought about something or someone and suddenly an email or a text message or even they appear? Your thoughts create a disturbance in the universal field of entanglement, which in turn moves and changes things around until an end result matches the thought pattern you sent out. With this in mind, it is important to exercise the self-discipline to pray daily to the Supreme Intelligence and ask for assistance in creating strength of character for yourself and everybody else. You can also pray to people and animals that have passed on and become energy in the field. These entities make themselves known to you the second you think of them. Knowing that everything is connected via thought, it also makes sense that every organism everywhere is in perpetual quantum communication via the zero point field. To understand the true nature of the Universe, think in terms of energy, frequency, vibration, and connection. What you 'think' has a powerful effect on what actually takes place. There have been many experiments carried out to prove this theory. The placebo effect is one prime example. What you believe to be true has the power to physically change your biology. The placebo effect is measurable, observable, and thanks to the power of your mind, workable.

The power of thought can also be measured by the effect of consciousness and intention directed at water. Many years ago, I came across the experiments of Masaru Emoto. In 1994, Masaru decided to freeze water and observe the frozen crystals with a microscope. The results were consistent in that positive intentions produced symmetric, well-formed, aesthetically pleasing frozen water crystals. Masaru observed crystals from plain tap water, river water, and lake water. The tap water did not create any beautiful crystals, nor did the rivers or lakes near big cities. Not surprisingly, the water from rivers and lakes where water is kept pristine and free from development produced the most beautiful crystals with each one having its own artistry and uniqueness. The experiments were carried out in various ways. The crystals were observed after exposing the water to letters, pictures, music, and prayer. The results were consistent in that beautiful crystals were always formed after exposing the water to kind words, calming music, and positive prayer. On the other hand, it was observed that the crystals were disfigured when the water was exposed to words of hate, abuse, and loud aggressive music. When you take into consideration the fact that your body is made up of roughly 70% water, it is clear that your thoughts and your prayers actually do effect your biology. Now is the time to begin the self-disciplined practise of 'prayer' and monitor the thoughts that can create disfigurement, unease, and disease in your physical body.

I am self-disciplined

4 Humility

Your soul is the divine part of you that initiates your desire to choose both the things you 'want' and the experiences you 'need'. Your soul navigates your life and prompts you to move in the direction that is best for your learning and growth. It is the part of you that guides you, speaks to your conscience, and 'enforces' the agenda of building your character. I often hear people say that they do not pray and have no belief in any type of 'God'. Many people think that praying must include a priest and a church and if they are not religious, they cannot imagine doing such a thing. What I know to be true is that everybody begins to pray when they are in the pits of anguish even if it is to their own soul via

51

thoughts of 'hope' or 'imploring'. The first thing people say when they are in a life-threatening situation is – 'God help me'. Your mind and heart need to 'generate' hope and faith whereas your soul is the part of you that is already 'knowing' that everything is exactly as it should be. Your soul is all that is and all that ever can be. It needs nothing added. It is perfect love and pure energy made manifest through you. Being humble 'feeds' your soul. Arrogance does not lead you to your soul but rather to your ego-mind. Having too much pride will also take you away from enlightenment. Returning to humility and bringing awareness to the ego and all of its trickery will help you to reach consciousness. You can do this by paying close attention to your thoughts. The part of you that pays attention to your thoughts is your 'higher-self' – consciousness, mindfulness, and your 'inner-witness' or your 'mind's-eye'. The more you are able to exercise this part of yourself, the more conscious and aware you will become.

Like any habit, consciousness develops over time. Once this practise is established, you will have mastered mindfulness. Aristotle said *"We are what we repeatedly do. Excellence then, is not an act, but a habit"*. Success does not happen overnight. Many people begin new things, embrace new ideas, and vow to make changes but before long, they are back to their default position. This happens to me a lot and I have to constantly remind myself to continue building strength of character in every situation that arises in my life. The reason for slipping back to 'old ways' is the absence of new replacing habits. Before you attempt to create a new habit, first determine what it is you want to change or add to yourself and be very clear around why you want to do this and then set in motion a plan as to how you are going to do it. Put some 'triggers' in place. When I made the conscious choice to become more 'mindful', I changed my watch from my left wrist to my right wrist. I created a physical sensation to 'remind' me to be mindful. Every time I felt my watch, I became present, aware, and mindful. I then asked myself "What was I thinking just now"? This helped me to become more in touch with my higher-self and expand my awareness. The more often I did this, the more this part of me started to come to the front of my psyche and I began to 'detach' from the drama that was happening in my life. I started to see and act above it and I found myself identifying with it less and less. Drama is like a vacuum that sucks you in and spins you around until you are so caught up, you cannot break free and you become miserably unconscious and disillusioned.

Pretension, extended pride, and smugness are the opposites of humility. Your ego is presumptuous and brass when it comes to right and wrong. Your ego-mind hates to be wrong and rarely admits when it is. It is hard to admit being wrong and harder still to arrive at being sorry. Egos are fragile. To your ego, forgiveness is an F-word. While your ego needs to work hard at generating 'forgiveness', your soul has no one to forgive because nobody can do it wrong. Everything that happens to you in your life is for growth and evolution. While your ego judges and condemns others, your soul is love and oneness. Your soul is most expressed when your ego is dissolved, when the frequency is turned down, and you become centred and inner-focused. Your soul can only be known through stillness, meditation, reflection, and prayer. Most people are way too busy, running around, frantic with life, and give very little time to their soul development. They go on retreat for a week and re-connect, return to life, and vow to continue the practise until the next distraction comes along and kidnaps their intention. If you think about the ending of your life, I suspect that the first fear and the saddest thought that comes to mind relates to the people you love and the realisation that you would leave them behind. Your soul is purity evidenced through your ability to love yourself and others. Your soul strives to help you master your mind and reach consciousness. It has a direct connection to your mind through your heart, your intuition, and your profound knowing. Your soul dominates your mind and is far more powerful than the structures of your ego or the concepts and illusions you attach to. Remain humble in knowing that you are powerful beyond measure and that your sheer existence will change the overall outcome of humanity, ultimately reshaping the entire future of the Universe and all that is.

I am humble

5 Encouragement

There is no such thing as 'impossible'. The word impossible is simply a dare to do whatever it is that is deemed impossible. Impossible is not a word in the language of the soul. Your soul comes from a dimension where impossible does not exist and you must not believe that it does. Impossible is temporary whereas possible is permanent. Your soul is the power of encouragement that outranks absurd, crazy, and ridiculous. Your soul takes you to new levels, moves you out of your current reality, and introduces you to your unseen, untapped, and unrivalled potential. There are no limits, no bounds, no restrictions to what you can touch, who you can be, or what you can become. You are immense, immeasurable, and endless when you allow the power of your soul to guide you and assist you toward the things you want; the things you cannot yet see or envision. When you spark an idea, wish, or desire, your soul ignites it and burns it into a reality that your ego-mind can receive. Your soul creates desire-thoughts in your mind and then calls on the power of the Universe, and the blessing of the Supreme Intelligence to deliver them to you so that you can contribute to the movement of ultimate creativity and infinite invention. The collective force of creativity requires the input of each and every person to add to universal creation. It is your mission to create your life, find your joy, prosper and thrive. Your soul insists upon it.

Your soul encourages confidence in you. Confident people are able to inspire confidence in others, their peers, bosses, customers, family, and friends. Gaining the confidence of other people is the first step in moving toward ultimate 'success'. Confident people exude this strength in their body language, speech, and choice of words, behaviour, and actions. Confident people do what is right, even if other people disagree, criticise, or mock them. Confidence is added to you when you live 'soulfully'. People who have a belief in something larger and more powerful than themselves are able to take risks, step outside of their comfort zone, and hand over control of their lives to the loving force that answers their prayers. Your soul determines what your challenges will be in this lifetime and you are never given a challenge you cannot pass through. You are always provided with answers through your wisdom, and given the help required to guide you along your way. When one option shuts down, another one opens up, and you are never given more than you can handle. Every problem comes with a solution taped to the back of it. Turn the problem over to the Supreme Intelligence and ask for this highest form of intelligence to lead you, instruct, and supervise you. When you doubt your ability to cope or succeed, ask your soul for help in the form of soul advice and then listen to your intuitive voice for the encouragement you need.

I am encouragement

6 Wisdom

The concept of 'totems' has been known throughout the world since the earliest days of Greek Mythology. According to Native Americans, a totem is a spirit being, sacred object, or a 'symbol' of the person. Animal guides, also called spirit guides or power animals come in and out of your life depending on the direction you are heading or the 'lessons' and 'challenges' you need to complete during your lifetime. Western culture has become 'detached' from spirituality, mysticism, and soulful living. You must reconnect and open your soul. Have you ever found yourself drawn to or fascinated by an animal, reptile, bird, or insect? The Supreme Intelligence and your 'spirit guides' cannot flick you a text message. At least not directly, they may through another person or 'vessel'. They use more subtle avenues such as 'signs', 'symbols', and 'synchronicity'. For example, I am currently writing this book, and as you know, I used the analogy of 'Two Ingredient Pancakes' to help you understand the concept. By 'co-incidence', a minute ago I opened a magazine and came across a recipe for 'Pancakes with Bananas & Hot Pecan Sauce'. This alone is probably not so convincing but I have learnt to notice more closely. The words 'pancakes' and 'bananas' got my attention. I have learnt how the Universe communicates with me. This full-page recipe has some pertinent words splashed across it. It says at the top 'You've worked hard this week – treat yourself to a little weekend decadence!' The Universe knows that I associate hard work with treating myself – it is sending me a pat on the back for my work on this book so far. The recipe also says 'Makes Eight'. Of course 'eight' is my favourite number. Everything good that comes to me has an eight in it, plane seats, dates, phone numbers, room numbers, ticket numbers, and even my favourite symbol – infinity, is an eight on its side. Put it all together and it translates to this – 'banana pancakes' – the analogy I have used, 'you've worked hard' – your work is appreciated, 'this book you are writing is going to be an eight' – the Universe is on my side, helping me, and sending me the wisdom and motivation I need. If the recipe had been 'blueberry muffins', 'makes twelve', I would not have looked twice. I know from experience that this message was meant for me and this sort of thing happens for me and for you ALL the time, always accurate, always meaningful, but ONLY when you allow yourself to be governed by your soul.

If you do not already have one, ask the Supreme Intelligence to send you a totem via a dream, vision, or repetitive sighting. You may start to see eagles, snakes, butterflies, or dolphins – something from the air, water, or land, a reptile, or an insect. When you recognise your totem, you can go to **www.whats-your-sign.com** to find out what it represents and bear in mind that the meaning you give it is always the most correct interpretation. My totem is the 'owl', which represents 'wisdom'. I see owls everywhere. People gift me owls. I have clothes, scarves, and jewellery with owl designs. I see them when I travel to other countries. I see them when I drive at night. They show up in my life to assure me that I am right where I am meant to be and that I need to continue my personal development and expand my virtue of wisdom. I received my very first owl gift (a beautiful white ceramic owl) from a friend I needed to move on from. She gave me a beautiful gift and taught me some valuable lessons, especially the importance of forgiveness with compassion. After reading Dr Phil's 'The Life Code', I now choose 'wisely' who my close friends will be. I have learnt to 'qualify' people and never give anyone the 'benefit of the doubt'. Your intuition is NEVER wrong. If you are doubtful of someone, it is because they are out of alignment with you. What signs, symbols, songs, words, phrases, colours, patterns, and totems show up in your life? Ask your soul to inform you of their meaning and reveal to you their guidance. Hone your skills for reading the language of the Supreme Intelligence and following directions from the Universe. The Universe uses images, pictures, photos, music, lyrics, nature, random events, circumstances, and occurrences. If you 'think' it is meant for you then it is. Do not doubt it. You are very special to the Supreme Intelligence and mountains will be moved for you. The love for you is as if nobody else exists. You are unique. There is only one 'you'. When you ask for help, every atom in existence answers the call. You can never ask for too much. Most people have no idea how powerful they are and no idea how relevant they are to the endless creation of life. Everything you ever need is already yours and every answer to every question is already contained in your soul's infinite wisdom.

I am wisdom

7 True-Gratitude

There are times when it feels like everything falls apart before it eventually comes together. During these times, feeling and expressing gratitude is a big undertaking. The rule with gratitude is that it needs to be authentic. True gratitude needs to bypass your ego and come from your soul. It requires a more potent sense of appreciation and acknowledgement. Grateful to be alive is soul driven recognition. Grateful for my shiny new car is ego driven self-praise. True gratitude needs no connecting 'object'. It just is, all on its own. There is gratitude at the mind level, at the heart level, and at the soul level. The soul 'is' gratitude already in the recognition and experience of existence. The heart 'feels' gratitude for health, wellbeing, and love. The mind 'chooses' gratitude for 'stuff' and is especially grateful when it is getting more stuff. The mind uses gratitude as a tool, a shovel for digging a bigger hole into 'what's here for me?' The heart feels gratitude for what is not being taken away and often transforms this gratitude into 'relief'. The soul is gratitude incarnate because it is a part of eternity. Expressing gratitude on all levels is good practise and serves an important purpose. Be clear where your gratitude is coming from because like attracts like and living a quality life requires you to be conscious on all three levels. Be grateful for the beauty you see in your life and grateful for the hope and joy you feel in your heart. Be especially grateful for the peace and grace you carry in your soul for this gratitude is the one you need to amplify. This true-gratitude carries your potential to change yourself and change the world.

One of the best ways to deepen gratitude and build strength of character is through the method of self-reflection and self-examination. The practise of self-reflection goes back many centuries and is rooted in the world's great spiritual traditions. Genuine self-reflection affects so many aspects of your life – the presence of gratitude, your relationships, the degree of judgement you have about other people's faults, your mental health, lifestyle choices, investment decisions, even your faith in the Supreme Intelligence. Self-reflection is not easy and your ego-mind is resistant to it and afraid of it. **'Naikan'** is a Japanese word that means 'inside looking', 'introspection', or 'seeing oneself with the mind's-eye'. Nai = inside and Kan = looking. Naikan is a structured method of self-reflection that helps you understand yourself, your relationships, and the nature of your existence. **Yoshimoto Ishin**, a devout Buddhist of the Jodo Shinsu set in Japan developed Naikan. As a young man, Yoshimoto engaged in the practise of 'Mishirabe' involving sensory deprivation through dwelling in a dark cave without food, water, or sleep. Lucky for us, he later developed Naikan as a less difficult and less extreme method. I personally am not a fan of the dark cave idea but I am in awe of people who undertake such devout commitments. I have visited Japan many times and I am always touched by how humble, polite, and grateful the Japanese people are. Leo Tolstoy said *"Man need only divert his attention from searching for the solution to external questions and pose the one, true **inner** question of how he should lead his life, and all the **external** questions will be resolved in the best possible way"*.

The Naikan method of self-reflection asks that you quietly reflect on the following three questions –

'What have I received?'
'What have I given?'
'What troubles and difficulty have I caused?'

True self-reflection requires the courage and confidence to look within and ask the hard questions. Question one is relatively easy as I am sure you can recall what you have received from a person, circumstance, or event. Question two is also quite painless as I am sure you can recall what you have given. Question three is the tricky one because most people focus on the troubles and difficulties others have caused them. I was guilty of reflecting on the hurt others had caused me until I realised that my growth would only come from asking myself what troubles and difficulties I myself had caused. My ego-mind squirmed like a slug in salt at having to do this exercise but it healed me and helped me to forgive and let-go. I imagine your ego-mind too will find it much easier to notice other people's bad behaviour, shortcomings, and failures. Children start 'dobbing' on other kids from an early age. Let's face it, it is delightful when somebody else is wrong, somebody else screws up, or somebody else is in trouble. Your ego-mind loves to be right and works hard at staying out of the firing line. If somebody else is in the spotlight, it means you are free to go. It takes strength of character to ask what you have done, said, or thought that has caused difficulty for another person. A negative thought, a disapproving look, a harsh word, a judgement, or a small piece of gossip is enough to cause trouble in another person's life. Don't ever underestimate what your judgemental opinion, criticism, or character assassination of somebody else can do to them or cause for them. When you truly look at yourself and accept responsibility for the times you have not been perfect or been less than kind, you can at least feel proud that you have the willingness, readiness, and fortitude to admit it, the honesty to see it, and the gratitude to divert your attention across to the intimate challenge of deep self-reflection.

I am truly grateful

Ingredients

2. Eggs – Similar to the shell of an egg, your outer ego is very fragile and delicate. You need to softly crack it open to get to the good stuff. The white of the egg represents your body (heart and emotions) and the need to be transparent, pure, and clean. The yolk of the egg represents your soul – the gold in the middle of who you are, rich and fertile, found only when the ego is carefully broken, gently opened, and lovingly exposed.

Crack-open your mind, body, and soul to establish 'knowledge of self'

Open your mind

Your mind is a powerful tool that can also sabotage and hobble your progress. Training your mind to open and expand is integral to Holifest. Narrow, negative thinking dis-empowers your mind and inhibits your ability to create and attract. Conflict with others often comes about through failing to see another person's perspective. Ask yourself what it must be like for them. Reflect on how they could be seeing things and what may be important to them. Broadening your perspective and giving more consideration to what other people want will ultimately help you achieve your own desires and success. The real secret to getting something you want is to first give it away. If you want more money in your life, be generous with what you have. If you want more happiness in your life, make it your mission to make other people happy. According to the law of creation, *'as you sow, so shall you reap'*. Staying present, conscious, and practising mindfulness is an additive to Holifest. Think of your mind as a large apartment with a mezzanine level where you can stand and 'observe' everything that is going on down below. Become the 'witness' of your thoughts and practise being 'spectator' of what comes into your mind. The part of you that becomes a 'bystander' is called 'consciousness'. Having this ability to observe your repetitive thoughts and detect and examine what your ego-mind 'thinks' is another element to Holifest.

Perspective

Following instructions and complying with a narrow view of how things 'must' be done is 'mindless'. Seeing everything from a single perspective is limiting and restricting. Try to stay open to creating brand new 'mind-sets'. Try to avoid 'categorising' everything according to the past categories you once created. Instead, create new categories and allow things to reveal themselves to you. For example, not all motorbike riders are tough, tattooed, troublemakers, even though people may 'categorise' them this way. BACA for example is a group of 'bikies' who give up their spare time to protect abused children. If you categorise bikies as deviates, then these 'bikies' require a new category. Loosen the ligaments of your mind and stretch it out so that you can create new categories and explore new possibilities. Elasticise the 'premature cognitive commitments' you made in the past when you stubbornly made up your mind about what you did and did not like. Start to broaden your perspective and try things out for a second time. Embrace new ideas, try new things, and be open to changing your mind. Look at things like they are 'unusual' rather than 'familiar'. Question everything you have ever thought about anything and query your limiting 'mind-sets'. You do not have to be governed by rules and routines. People who break the rules have more charisma than those who are too afraid to step out of the square. Break the rules, not the 'law'. Having the ability to see things from another person's perspective is a trait that is common in successful people. *We do not see things as they are; we see things as we are.* To really understand what motivates others and to grasp why they react and behave the way they do is the only way to develop the important quality of empathy. Having empathy and compassion for others immediately sets you apart from the crowd. In business particularly, nobody really cares too much about what you want. People are far more concerned with what they want and how what you want will ultimately affect them. In order to be successful, you need to be able to see what other people need and then go about creating solutions to their problems. The only way to do this is to start to see things from their perspective not just from yours. If you can develop the skill and practise of seeing things from other people's perspectives, you will add to your character and finally succeed where others have failed.

Mindfulness and Presence

The average person is mindless around 95% of the time. Your thoughts are on a mission to take you either into the future or back to the past. When you move through your day, most of the time, you are running on 'auto-pilot'. The tasks you are familiar with such as driving your car or cleaning your teeth are handed over to your unconscious mind. They no longer require your conscious mind or even your presence. In other words, these tasks are carried out without your conscious awareness. Have you ever arrived somewhere without having remembered the journey? Have you looked for something you are already holding or wearing? This happens because you are functioning mindlessly and relying on your unconscious. This is not the way to go forth and Holifest. Mindfulness is the ability to stay present and notice new things. Mindfulness is being able to pay 100% attention to the task you are doing. Becoming 'engaged' in what you are doing and noticing the steps, the sensations, and the surroundings is what you need to do to become more mindful. Every time you turn on a light, do it mindfully. Actually 'think' about doing it, feel your finger on the switch, look at the switch, and give it your full attention, and then watch carefully as the light explodes the darkness. If you start to do this, you will no longer leave home wondering if you left the oven on and you will begin to live in the 'now', in 'present time', in what I call the 'immediate'.

Become the observer and master of your mind so that you can 'choose' the thoughts you are going to accept and absorb. Martin Seligman, the founder of Positive Psychology says that the human brain is wired to be negative. In the past, our brains needed to be alert to danger in order to survive. There was not a lot of time for daydreaming or you would become easy prey for a passing lion. For the purpose of survival, your brain has learnt to 'prioritise' negative information rather than positive. We tend to pay more attention to criticism and reproach than to praise and approval. Research shows that people experience more negative emotion from losing money than positive emotion from gaining money. This is why something 'bad' happening can wipe out positive emotions and something 'good' happening does not have the same power to wipe out negative emotions. In other words, if your partner comes home in a bad mood, you will more readily engage in a bad mood yourself. By comparison, if your partner comes home in a good mood and finds you in a bad mood, your bad mood is less likely to alter and before long, to your great victory, your partner will join you and you will both be in a bad mood together. It is far easier to be 'put' in a bad mood than a 'good' mood. Martin Seligman states that negative emotions hold the power to 'trump' positive emotions. Your job is to keep check on negative emotions and learn to 'amplify' the positives.

Feel your body

Your physical body is both a vehicle and a sanctuary. Your body is a precious gift that is worthy of your respect. Whilst your body moves you around and sustains a physical life for you, it also works with you, your spirit, and your soul to operate your life and skipper your very existence in the physical realm. Your body is constantly giving you feedback, analysing data, and reacting to stimulus to assist you in navigating your life through your senses and your divine intelligent intuition. If you are ever stuck on making a decision, your body will hold the answer as can be experienced through kinesiology, the holistic health discipline that uses muscle monitoring to access information. Treating your body with love and appreciation is paramount to having a quality relationship with your physical form. Like all relationships, it is built on value, acceptance, and often forgiveness. The body you have is perfect for you in this lifetime and serves you on every level. Your physical appearance and unique good looks are designed just for you. Focus on the features you like and always make the most of yourself. Present yourself to the world with confidence and pride. Do not ever put yourself down. Be mindful of how you preserve the health and wellbeing of your physical body. Learn how to work with the feelings and sensations your body generates for a more profound understanding of life. If you feel that your body has 'let you down' at any time through injury or illness, know that the end goal is to assist you in building strength of character, developing endurance, and increasing stamina.

Fear

Humans are born with only two fears – the fear of loud noises and the fear of falling. All other fears are learned or inherited. They exist in your mind, but to you, they are real. Trying to stop yourself from experiencing fear is a fruitless exercise and totally unnecessary. Instead, embrace your fears and rewire yourself for positivity. Filter out some of the automatic, habitually ingrained fear-based thinking that sabotages your life and produces stress and anxiety. The first step is to invite your fears in so that you can meet them face-to-face and look them straight in the eye. Everybody has their own view about themselves, others, the world, and how it all works. These views or perceptions control what you do without you even being aware of it. Many of your fears and beliefs are subconscious however they guide and drive your emotional responses to the circumstances and events that take place in your life. It is important to examine your fears and beliefs in order to change any negative thinking. Your thinking forms your habits, and your habits eventually shape who you are. What limiting beliefs do you hold about yourself or your life? For example, do you believe that this world has limited resources and there is not enough to go around? Do you believe that if you succeed, you will be taking something away from somebody else? Do you believe that you are a place getter rather than a winner? Do you believe that you need to control what happens in order to feel safe and secure? Do you believe that you are less important than the next person? When you start to scrutinize your fears and beliefs, you then have the opportunity to decide how much hold they are going to have over you or not. Out of control fears will hold you back. You are stronger than your fears. Think about a fear you are holding right now and take it through the following three steps:

1 Ask yourself – 'What is the worst that can happen'?

When you are anxious about something, be it work, a deadline, a conflict, a relationship, or a decision, it helps to take a deep breath and then walk your mind through the worst-case scenario. Imagine all of the possibilities and outcomes you most dread and ask yourself if it is something you could live with or live through? Even if your upcoming public speaking engagement, presentation, or the cold call you have to make goes horribly wrong, chances are that you will survive. Losing your job or a client is not the end of the world. The times in my life when things have been taken away, something bigger, better, and more suited has always replaced them. At the time, it can feel like the Universe is stripping you down with ruthless indifference but the most challenging times call for the most perseverance, the deepest faith, and the greatest hope. Life will ensure you have highs and lows. Dale Carnegie said *"Most of the important things in the world have been accomplished by people who have kept on trying when there seemed to be no hope at all"*. When things go 'wrong', soothe yourself and visualise the result you want rather than the result you do not want. Focusing for too long on what you do not want will inevitably bring that experience closer to you.

2 Confront your fear head on:

Avoiding fear only gives it more power over you. Susan Jeffers said *"Feel the fear and do It anyway"*. Each time a fear is examined and defied, it becomes easier to cope with new fears and concerns. Confronting your fear desensitises you and dissolves the fear itself. The next time the fear presents, it has less power over you, and then in the end, it is no longer a problem. Roosevelt said, *"So, first of all, let me assert my firm belief that the only thing we have to fear is ... fear itself"*. Imagined fears tend to be much worse than reality. Fear is like a bully. When you stand and confront it, it cowers away, afraid of itself, and terrified you will soon realise that it does not even exist. If you fear something, 'do it'. If you fear flying then board more planes. If you fear public speaking then join Toastmasters. If you fear heights then take the elevator to the top. The only way to quash your fear is to confront it. Choose a support person or join a group if you cannot do it alone but find a way to do it. Marianne Williamson said *"Love is what we were born with. Fear is what we learned here"*. I have learnt to love my fear, strengthen the virtue that matches it, and pray for help, solutions, and answers. I feel fear before I speak in public and before I jump my horse but I have consciously transformed that fear into excitement, motivation, and challenge instead. If it weren't scary, it would not be thrilling. Let your fears thrill you rather than paralyse you. Tell yourself that you are excited rather than afraid.

3 Share it:

Sharing your fear with another person halves its power, effect, and ability to intimidate. Talk about your fears with a trusted partner, relative, counsellor, or friend. Often when you talk through your fears, you will expose and then question the influence they have over you and start to see that it is all in your shadow-imagination. Fear leads to anxiety and although most people view anxiety as a negative experience, there can be some benefits to it if you change your mind-set about what anxiety really is. If you experience anxiety as an ally, you will be less likely to 'resist' it, which in turn only amplifies and escalates it. There is nothing more debilitating than being anxious about being anxious. Instead, your anxiety can be a type of 'super-force' that takes over you and makes you more dynamic, more potent, and vigorous. You can view it as something to be subdued and 'tamed' rather than a 'fault' in you that needs to be 'corrected'. Anxiety can help you make better decisions. The absence of anxiety can often mean that you do not care. People who have suffered the type of damage to their brain that prevents them from experiencing 'anxiety' or 'fear' behave impulsively, become socially inept, and have a total disregard for their future and their safety. Anxiety and logic help you make sound decisions and can enhance your ability to pay attention to relevant information. Reasonable and manageable levels of anxiety can help you perform better and successfully rise to the challenge.

Feelings

Using your emotions as a source of wisdom is another part of Holifest. You have an internal navigation device installed in your heart. I call this your 'heart-ellite' instead of 'sat-ellite' navigation system. It is like a satellite streaming directions to your heart. This is your body's 'tool' for 'sensing' where you are at and where you are meant to be going. Your body communicates and guides you through your feelings and emotions. You will have physical reactions to circumstances and events or you will experience a range of emotions, which are responses and creations. Emotions are part of your complex inner make-up. They respond to your thoughts and beliefs. Emotions can either be self generated or 'inherited'. Working exclusively on changing your thoughts is counterproductive. A thought-based approach dismisses the connection to how you are really feeling as opposed to how you think you are feeling or worse still, how you think you are 'supposed' to be or 'expected' to be feeling. Use your feelings for guidance. They will point you toward the virtue you need to ripen. Open your heart and practise compassion for others. You can achieve this by teaching, mentoring, educating, and providing personal assistance. Giving your time and energy is much more valuable than giving your money. People who live a life of service strengthen their hearts and their souls. Philanthropy is a fast track way to wellbeing. Committing to an altruistic endeavour will amplify your Holifest immensely. Explore charities and look into world issues, community support programs, caring for the elderly or homeless. The more you give of yourself and the more you are of service to others, the happier and more contented you will be. This has been proven many times over through experience and through psychological studies.

Conflict

At times there will be conflict between what you think and what you feel. The outcome of this rivalry will ultimately instruct you and show you the way. You are the only person with the consciousness to perceive your thoughts and feel your feelings. Nobody else can adequately 'advise' you on what to do. They can however be of assistance in reflecting back to you your thoughts and feelings. My friend Sue has always asked "How much did you pay for that advice"? People are usually enthusiastic about giving you their well-meaning 'free' advice but they could suggest that you do something that is not good for you. Often your heart and mind are in conflict in order to create the opportunity for you to get in touch with your 'instinctual knowing'. Ask your heart which direction your heart-ellite navigation system is telling you to go. More often than not, the 'right' way is the 'hardest' way. Your ego likes shortcuts and smooth roads whereas your heart and soul like the round scenic tour with its windy bends, dangerous drops, and wild adventures. People tend to like things to be clear-cut, either this way or that, all or nothing, directions falling from the sky. They seek definitive conclusions but life operates on a grey scale and there are many different aspects to any one situation or opportunity. Be patient when you are juggling conflicting thoughts and feelings. Often conflicting interests and loyalties will accompany this 'dilemma-state'. Pay attention to how your desires affect you and what repercussions or consequences they will have on yourself and others. Observe what you 'think' and also how you 'feel'. Often these inconsistencies show up to give you time or to allow the Universe to shuffle and move things in your favour and for your highest good. Conflict often arises when your mind chooses something that is not right for your soul. You may 'think' that you want that job, relationship, or interstate move but you cannot see the big picture. The Universe is a large crystal ball held in the hand of the Supreme Intelligence that can see your future. If you ignore your 'intuition' that is the 'voice command' from your heart-ellite navigation system, you will come to a grinding halt. You will find yourself saying "I don't know what to do". When this happens, just wait, and when in doubt, don't. Time will reveal more to you, circumstances will change, events will unfold, conditions will alter, and the way will become clear and known. Pray for the answer and then just sit it out until your inner conflict resolves itself and is replaced with a confident steady 'knowing'.

Fold into your soul

Regardless of your belief system or religious denomination, there is one universal truth that points to some type of 'creator'. The 'Supreme Intelligence' that created this Universe is without gender, form, creed, or colour. No religious or spiritual teacher would deny this fundamental truth. The Supreme Intelligence is 'oneness' and you are one with it as you are with everything and everyone else. Within your mind, body, and soul, you have the virtues and attributes of the Supreme Intelligence. You are a part of it and its spirit is also your spirit. Your soul is the highest, most divine aspect of who you are and the truest form of your core being. It is the eternal part of you that supersedes death. It is devoid of all elements of human personality and character. It is a direct fragment of the divine creator, the Supreme Intelligence. Your soul is perfect and universal in all aspects. It directs your human character for the purpose of turning darkness into light, transforming weakness into strength, and beckoning your ego to step aside so that you once again unite with the great power of your absolute divinity. Your soul is far more powerful than your ego-mind yet it is quieter and subtler – the great dichotomy. It is allied with your heart and controls your conscience and your consciousness. The game of life uses your ego-mind to take you away from your soul until the pain becomes so intense that you want nothing more than to find your way back. Many people even contemplate suicide in order to return to spirit life and free themselves from the arduous task of being human. Life is the drama you engage in while knowing that it is all an illusion. The real you is more powerful than you can imagine, more conscious and aware than you will ever know, and more immortal than you can comprehend. Your soul is enmeshed with the spirit that breathes life into you. When you ignore instructions from your soul and align yourself with your shadow emotions, your judgements, anger, resentment, and resistance, your spirit dims and your body becomes dis-eased. Illness is often a result of dismissing your intuition and attaching to your ego-mind with all its drama and falseness. Your spirit is your energy, life force, chi, and breath. It is infinite, eternal, and servant to your soul.

Your soul drives and governs your life and sends destinations of challenge, hardship, and adversity for your spiritual growth to your heart-ellite navigation system. Your soul uses your heart to direct you toward your greatest potential within the human experience. Your soul has an agenda that your ego is bound to resist and works within the parameters of 'build you up' and 'make you strong'. Your ego-mind has no great desire to strengthen other than to guarantee your progress in the material world. Your ego likes to make you strong because strength wins the game of 'survival of the fittest'. Your ego likes you to move through life set on 'cruise' control where everything lines up and comes your way with ease and flow. Your ego does not like the program your soul has in store for you. Your soul is set on course to take you home, back to the Supreme Intelligence where love and light are your masters. Your soul will do whatever it takes to guide you there and that's why bad things happen to good people. When your ego is crushed and your heart is broken, you have no choice but to turn to your spirit and call on the power of your soul. Your spirit will feed you the will to continue, to rise, to breathe, and move your body into another day. The only way you can endure the blow that comes from the death of someone or something that you love, cherish, or hold dear, (everything that ends is a death), is to dive into the resources of your soul. The seven virtues of your soul are built to sustain you when you suffer, when tragedy strikes, and when you are at your lowest point. At the bottom of the well, in your deepest despair, you will find the **assertiveness** to command your spirit to fight for you. You will develop the **determination** to survive and heal. You will summon the **self-discipline** to pray for the strength, help, and support you need to get you through. You will obtain the **humility** to accept that you do not control your life and you will acknowledge that the agenda laid out for you is beyond your human comprehension. You will establish the soulful **encouragement** you need through your faith to look forward and imagine a brighter future. You will gather the **wisdom** to know that things happen for reasons you may or may not ever discover but you know without a doubt that everything eventually works out for the greater good. Finally, you will connect with the **true-gratitude** your soul radiates for being human and living in the dimension that can only be experienced through the flesh, through the mind, feelings, emotions, and the connection of love between people, nature, and all things made Holifest.

Inspiration

Your mind communicates with you via your thoughts whereas your soul communicates with you via your intuition. Inspiration comes from the Supreme Intelligence, through your soul, via your intuition. Inspiration is the guiding hand of the Supreme Intelligence. It cannot be ignored or discounted. To do so would be like dying a slow death of spiritual and creative starvation. Inspiration starts gently and then becomes a nagging spur in your heart, coaxing you, beckoning to the very fibre of your being to listen, follow, and create. Ignoring inspiration and rejecting the call of your soul is torture to your wellbeing and murder to your Holifest. Inspiration is like water to a plant, milk to a baby, oxygen to your lungs. It is a 'force' that makes your life meaningful and purposeful. There will be times when you cannot act immediately and you will need to be patient and faithful but inspiration is in no rush. It selects you and 'marks' you for its purpose. The timing may be off or your idea not quite right but inspiration continues to show up attempting to match you to the brief. Inspiration that comes to you is meant for you. It calls to your talents, your abilities, your qualities, and it will keep calling until you answer. Inspiration will present sketches, ideas, and rough layouts until you give your approval. Inspiration is like a match, enticing and demanding you to strike it so that it can become a mighty raging fire of creativity. When your mind has co-operation from your heart and direction from your soul, you will effortlessly Holifest brilliant concepts into your next best creative conception.

Surrender

The need to be right and make someone else wrong is a priority for your ego but it does not make you popular. It is not so awesome to be right – even a watch with a flat battery is right twice a day. There is nothing wrong with being wrong. It is good for your ego-mind to humble itself and admit that it is not perfect. Saying 'sorry' or 'I am wrong' is like taking a vitamin pill for your ego. Needing to be right can fool you into thinking that you are the only person who knows the most effective way to tackle a task, problem, or challenge. This then leads to your expectation that others are going to follow 'your way' and bend their will to you. Needing to control people and situations will block your capacity to delegate and inhibit your trust in others. Surrendering control assigns the big stuff to the Supreme Intelligence, the highest form of intelligence and creativity to take over your life. Wouldn't you prefer the entity that created the entire omnipotent Universe to be the 'Director' of the movie that is the story of your life? I sure would. When you surrender everything you are grabbing onto and hand it all over, you can then relax and actually enjoy the journey while learning to move gently with the script for 'My amazing life'. Co-creation is the ultimate way to Holifest. Set the intention and then completely let go and natural flow will take over. Put your trust in creation and stick to your mantra. Everything is in place for your success. Yield and give way to the magic that happens when you step aside, move out of your own way, and trust in the Universe and the Supreme Intelligence that created it.

Method: The fundamentals of Holifest

The Short Cut Devil

Virtuous people strive for excellence in everything they do. They turn the 'mundane' into the 'muntastic'. They excel at all things and settle for nothing. They are not perfectionists yet they bring supremacy to every task, endeavour, and undertaking that comes their way. Your level of excellence will be for you to judge in the privacy of your own mind. Unless you are completing an assignment for somebody else, you are only accountable to your own personal benchmark for excellence. You could cut corners and nobody would know however you have your own conscience to argue with and justify your actions to. Your higher-self demands excellence and pops out of nowhere when the temptation to 'slacken-off' comes visiting. I was washing my Mini the other day and it came time to clean the wheels. Scrubbing tyre rims is one of my least favourite jobs. It always ends with black stains under my fingernails that scream 'wear gloves', but I never do. I am a bare hands kind of girl. My car has black rims so after a quick hose off they look relatively clean. Once the dust is removed, they have half a shine to them but

I know they aren't really done. I can always see the 'short-cut devil' out the corner of my eye waving his little red flag and raising his eyebrows at me. He growls in my conscience, loud enough for only me to hear. When I saw his beady little eyes, I dropped to my knees in the mud and scrubbed those rims, hosed them off, wiped my brow, and smiled defeat at that dirty little devil. Excellence wins again. Do not slacken off, do not short cut, and do not give in to the short-cut devil.

Doctor Doubt

Doctor Doubt is the physician of fear. He administers drugs of apprehension, disbelief, and uncertainty. He also has strong medication for non-deserving, unworthiness, and self-loathing. You know you need this doctor when you find yourself constantly checking the phone, emails, letterbox, and social media, worrying that it is not going to happen or you come down with a nasty dose of 'FOMO' (fear of missing out). Excess alcohol, drugs, and other destructive habits are evidence that you've seen the bad doctor. The only way to avoid Doctor Doubt is to take your homeopathic remedy. Your remedy is 'success'. It comes in a large jar of 'set yourself up' and the only side effects are creative, courageous, confident, and successful. Become your own private personal assistant and organise yourself. Create systems for the smooth running of all your affairs. Design a reward system for yourself where you can encourage your progress with treats and trinkets that help you value yourself and celebrate your success every step of the way. You deserve the best. You deserve to have your desires met with even more than you originally hoped for. You are a child of the

Supreme Intelligence and this 'parent' figure wants to see you happy and spoil you just like a parent who wants to indulge their child. The Supreme Intelligence wants you to receive your desires so stop throwing temper tantrums and start planning or you will find yourself sitting in Doctor Doubt's waiting room. Above all, be sure to remember that a virtue a day keeps the doctor away.

The Void

It can last for a fraction of a second or for many years, depending on the circumstances and your connection to will. This period is the hardest, most challenging part of Holifest. It is the empty, depressing, lonely 'gap' that appears in the creative process where there is a sense of nothingness, accompanied by helplessness, followed close behind by the dreadful sinking feeling of hopelessness. It is a time when life feels nothing like 'suc-cess' and a lot like 'suc-suck'. This Void however is a necessary step that must be taken. There is a fervent relationship between loneliness and creativity. This loneliness lodges itself in your heart and never fully leaves your psyche. It is felt more strongly in company than in solitude. Your pain body feeds on nothingness and binges on loneliness. This type of loneliness has been felt and experienced by many great artists and out of it, many great works of art have been born. Dorothy Day said *"We have all known the long loneliness"*. And Virginia Wolf wrote – *'these October days are to me a little strained and surrounded with silence. What I mean by this last word I do not know, since I have never stopped 'seeing' people ... No, it is not physical silence; it is some inner loneliness"*. This lonely silence is inseparable from the creative impulse, the creative process, and Holifest. The nothingness and loneliness of The Void requires you to stay true to yourself, hold onto your faith, and develop the unwavering belief that you truly deserve what you have asked for. During this time, the best approach is to focus your mind, heart, and soul on the mantra 'I am creative, courageous, confident, successful'. When Doctor Doubt comes knocking, and he will, the mantra will keep you well. It will help you to stay on course and move closer to your desires. When you feel like dropping your price or asking for less, or taking something you know to be inferior or second best, DO NOT. This is the time when all the wrong things show up. Don't get frustrated, instead be grateful that things are showing up at all and hold the faith that the right thing is on its way. Stay focused on your desires and do not sell yourself out just because you are worried or living close to the bone. The Void is testing you. It is like a black hole that will swallow you up if you walk too close to the slippery edge. Keep firmly planted in the immediate. Do not run off with fear. Stay and dance in The Void, accept what is, remain faithful, and say your mantra. Increase your virtues and look for ways to carry out random acts of kindness. Kindness toward others is the best way to 'a-void' The Void.

Limits and Less

Your sense of deserving is directly related to your self-worth, which is generated by your self-esteem. Nobody is born with high self-esteem. Self-esteem is built when you come to realise through experience and repetition that you can rely on yourself. It increases when you judge your character according to your intimate observation of yourself mixed with other people's responses to you. Self-esteem grows when you solve problems and create independence. When you know with certainty that you can meet your own needs and you do not 'long' for somebody else to complete you. Successful people are self-reliant, quiet achievers, who are confident in their own abilities and strengths. When you lack self-esteem, you start negotiating with yourself and you sell yourself short. You begin to think that you deserve less or you hear yourself say "that will do". Do not be fooled into thinking this Universe is small and that unless you get 'that' job or 'that' house, 'that' promotion, or 'that' partner, you will not find anything bigger, better, more suitable, or more magnificent. You are the only one who sets limits on what you are 'worthy' of so don't be tempted to down scale your expectations. The Universe is unlimited and the options are endless. During the Holifest process, less will always show up first. You will receive something that falls short, that does not quite fit or match. This is a test. Do not accept it and do not resent it. Be grateful that a result is emerging and simply pass over the limits and less until the real deal appears. Do not settle for second prize. Something perfectly suited that ticks every box is on its way. Hold on, you are not there yet. Your heart will tell you when its right and it will be better than you hoped for and more than you imagined with lashings of 'woo-hoo' on top.

Will Power

Will power is constantly flowing to you from the source – the will of the Supreme Intelligence – Supreme Will. It is your connection to this flow that fluctuates and falters. When you say you do not have enough will power to carry out a task or face a challenge, what you are really saying is that you have lost 'connection' to Supreme Will. Supreme Will is also your will because you are one and the same. This 'will power' is fed to and distributed by your soul and if you are not living soulfully, you will become disconnected, despondent, and depressed. When you log-out of your ego-mind and plug-in to your soul, you instantly re-connect with Supreme Will and find your will power once again. You can consciously make this connection through your mind using a prayer of asking, meditating, saying the mantra, or practising mindfulness. When you lose connection, it is because you have moved off your reason for being, you have stopped praying, and you have disconnected from your soul. You have become detached from the energy and lifeline that feeds will power to you and resuscitates your spirit. Instead you have connected to earth and lost touch with your 'higher-self'. Self-discipline through the power of prayer will always bring you back into alignment and re-connect you with Supreme Will. You can stay connected consciously by living your life serving and strengthening your soul. Your higher-self prompts you to live soulfully. It whispers softly behind your eyes reminding you that what you see on the outside is the smallest part of your life and what you give power to on the inside is your true reason for being and real purpose for existence. Like all forces, will power also has a shadow side, a de-motivator that undermines you and sabotages your every effort. I call this shadow – 'will powerless'.

Will Powerless

Carrying out obnoxious, hideous, repulsive tasks disarms and cancels out will powerless, the shadow side of will power. Quelling your will powerless builds and strengthens your connection to will power. Doing something yucky, disgusting, demotivating or unappealing every day will satisfy and keep your will powerless in line. You can clean the toilet, scrub the sink, remove spider webs, file your toenails, mop the floor, go on a public litter hunt, clean behind the lounge, wash the trash bin, empty the gutters, bleach the towels, polish your tyre rims, clean the grease trap, be kind to someone you don't like, sweep the pavement, pick up the dog poo, clean the dishwasher filters, or squeegee the windows. Do something unpleasant, boring or difficult and do it 'willingly' to strengthen your connection to will power. Anyone can do something pleasant and joyful but to do something unpleasant and do it gleefully and mindfully is a valuable discipline that will strengthen your connection to will power. If you find yourself resisting this suggestion, or justifying why you do not need to do it, then you will know that your connection to Supreme Will is currently weak and threatening to disconnect. Practise connecting with Supreme Will and use this divine will power to Holifest and avoid idling along in your life, constantly missing out on what you really want and truly deserve. Thomas Parker Boyd said *"**The will** is the keystone in the arch of human achievement. It is the culmination of our complex mental faculties. It is the power that rules minds, men, and nations"*. Your will comes straight from divine will when you connect through your soul.

Forgiveness

Forgiving somebody who has mentally or emotionally hurt you or physically harmed you is a bitter pill to swallow. People often mistake forgiveness as a gift to the other person but the truth is it is a gift to you. Anger and resentment burn a hole in your heart and often the other person doesn't think twice about it. Forgiveness requires you to self-reflect, identify who hurt you, and ask yourself how they were given the opportunity to do so. Did you let down your guard and give somebody the 'benefit of the doubt' or were you a powerless innocent victim? As soon as somebody comes along that requires you to give them the benefit of the doubt, take note that your intuition is warning you because it knows something that you do not yet know or do not want to know. Acknowledge and admit it if you are harnessing resentment. Do not fob it off and try to convince yourself that you are over it when your heart knows damn well that you aren't. Do not take the hurt personally. Often you are playing a part in somebody else's lesson and it has nothing to do with you. Begin to see the experience as a positive lesson for you. What have you endured? Have you learnt to cope with rejection, abandonment, betrayal, or humiliation? Have you overcome being a victim? These are all tasks that help you build strength of character. What has transformed in you? Have you developed compassion, reasoning, or the ability to let go, rise above it, and become more loving and wise for the future? Finally, you need to accept the experience and develop gratitude for the learning you have gained along with the resilience, stamina, and endurance this experience has enhanced in you.

Doing

Faith can move mountains, but do not be surprised if the Supreme Intelligence hands you a big fat shovel and asks you to start digging. 'Doing' with the help of your shovel and digging vigorously will see your mountain moved. While you are busy doing something constructive, meaningful, and worthwhile, the Universe is shifting mountains, relocating rivers, and altering canyons to bring your intention and desires to you. If you are in 'The Void' or experiencing indecision or confusion, simply start 'doing'. Plant a garden, paint a wall, wash the car, walk the dog, polish the silver, bake a cake, or shine your shoes. It doesn't matter what you do, just do something to keep your mind busy and give it something positive to focus on. While you are doing, say the mantra or hum a virtue. Work your body, blister your hands, and put your back into it. Hard work will not kill you, and it is no secret that hard work pays off. Thomas Edison said *"Opportunity is missed by most people because it is dressed in overalls and looks like work"*. Being active and productive lifts you to a higher vibration, a more powerful frequency than the one you radiate when you are sitting on the couch complaining about what has not happened yet to anyone who will listen. When you feel stuck and you don't know what to do, just do something. The action of 'doing' will generate the energy you need in and around you to change your current circumstances and transform your present situation into something much more Holifest.

Success

Most people associate success with dollars in the bank but real prosperity is associated with many different things. Success is accomplishment, achievement, and progress. It can be measured by happiness, freedom, inner peace, winning, or wellbeing. There is not much point to being rich and hoarding all your dollars and cents if you are not enjoying yourself, doing what you love, and blissed out on life. I know people who are extremely wealthy but nasty unhappy and others who live from hand to mouth yet crack a smile that can light up a room. Success is being able to ask for help. Needing assistance from others is not a failure. Successful people surround themselves with a supportive group of peers and professionals. The path that leads to success is a stairway. It is an uphill route, not a comfortable chairlift to the top. The only way to the peak of the mountain is to climb and that is where the panoramic view awaits you. Before you start ascending, get clear on what you are climbing for. What does success look like for you? Success could look like more time with your loved ones, freedom to choose, greater education, power to help, knowledge and skills, or changes taking place. Success is definitely found in strength of character. Determine your end goal before you start climbing. You have to know what you are working toward and why you want what you want. If you do not gain peace and happiness through success then it is not success at all. Success should benefit you and others; make you triumphant and victorious. It is a win, not a loss, and only you can weigh that up and measure it for yourself. Success often holds hands with failure. Successful people fail because they are attempting something, taking risks, and exploring new ways. Some people are so afraid of failing they don't even try. Don't be afraid. Be a successful person who sometimes fails on the journey to achieving. Be a successful person who never gives up, finds last minute stamina, and eventually arrives at the destination. You deserve to be a success.

The steps to Holifest

1) Decide what you want and set your intention

- Do you want more freedom, more money, less stress, a new home, more love, a romantic relationship, a promotion, more excitement, regular clients, more friends, a renovated body, a makeover, time off, personal space, a holiday, deeper spirituality, flexibility, a new car, a contract, some new clothes, increased fitness, an interview, a gig, a hit song, more work, a change, fame, popularity, resolved conflict, a child, healthier relationships, greater responsibility, better health, house extensions, new neighbours? There is an endless list of what you could want and everybody wants something.

2) Ask your heart why you want it and what is needed to get you there

- Log on to your heart-ellite navigation system to give you some directions. Where are you going? How do you arrive at what you want? What do you need to 'do'? Why is it important to you? Would you feel less of a person without it? Do you feel worthy? Can you survive without it? Are you afraid? Do you doubt yourself? Have you earned it? Are you craving it or longing for it? Are you being needy? Is your heart in alignment with what your mind is telling you? Scan your body for any sensations of fear, tension, anxiety, or emotional stress. Read the clues your body sends you.

3) Ask your soul if it is right for you

- Listen to your intuition. Be still and quiet to determine if you want what you want for all the right reasons and because it is going to add to you. Sometimes not getting what you want adds to you even more and your soul finds a different way to build your character. Your soul is only interested in becoming virtuous and experiencing the 'fullness' of life including all the things your ego does not like. Does this thing you want make you a better person? Does it help you to transform a shadow virtue? Does it honour you and add to the world in a positive way? Is it meant for you and are you meant for it? Does it keep you on track to becoming fulfilled and moving onto what you can become? If what you want is purely for your ego, or if it affects another person poorly, or if it is not going to improve you, it is not going to happen. You may not always know what is best for you but Supreme Intelligence does. Whatever you want has to benefit your soul and the Universe in some way. What you want has to build your strength of character and add to your virtues.

- Grab your faith and trust with both hands now. Stop checking the phone and waiting for the call. Stressing and 'needing' will only push what you want further away from you. There can be nothing you need that badly. Everything works out for you. It always has. You will get what you want and more. The Universe loves you and has moved everything to help you become bigger, better, and stronger. You are one Holifest closer to becoming the next best magnificent version of yourself. Now that you have decided what you want and you have gained permission from your heart, hand it over to your soul and say **"I let go. I let you."** This is the most important step of surrender, faith, and strength. Truly let go of the outcome. Your job is done here at this point. Your soul has intelligence beyond what your mind could imagine and wields power exceeding anything you know in existence. Let your soul rule your life and get back to the task of building virtues through developing strength of character. You are success made Holifest. You are ready to receive.

4) Endure the 'Void' and do not negotiate with 'Limits and Less'

- There will be a void or a delay in receiving what you want. You could experience this void for seconds, hours, days, weeks, or even years. This is the time when 'inferior' options will show up and present themselves to you. Look to your intuition via your heart and soul for guidance when this happens. Your conscience will tell you if you are selling out on yourself and attaching to something less than you deserve, settling for second best, or accepting 'that will do'. You will feel it in your heart as a type of 'sinking' feeling if what comes along is not aligned with your heart's desire. Always appreciate and feel grateful for what shows up in order to attract more but don't settle for anything below the mark. Go slow and remember to read the signs along the way. The Universe will make its plan known to you. Synchronicity will fire up and forces will explode to ensure the magic of Holifest happens.

5) Stay 'Mindful' and 'Do'

- Keep track of your thinking. Do not let sabotaging thoughts dance in your mind. Do a quick tango with them and send them spinning. Keep your mind present with mindfulness and engage with your higher-self to stay aware. You are close to receiving now and your mind will be trying its hardest to make you lose faith. Continue to be alert and determined so that you remain anchored in the 'immediate'. Get busy and work toward what you want. Do whatever it takes. Knock on doors, send out emails, and tidy your desk. Do, do, and just 'do' anything. It doesn't matter what you do, just get busy doing something constructive. Better still, do something for somebody else and the end result will be receiving what you want for yourself.

Holifest-ending

In conclusion, the soul purpose of your life is not for you to acquire a heap of 'stuff', amass a fortune that you cannot take with you, or fight your way to the top. If you happen to do all of this and still build strength of character, find inner peace, and live mindfully while offering yourself up for service to the world, then you need to be writing a big fat book on how this has been achieved. If your priority is 'what can I get' rather than 'what can I give' then it is not going to work out well for you in the end. Your soul purpose is for you to become someone more than you are right now. It is to learn how to use the power and force of your mind to honour your soul and evolve to fulfillment while expanding your capacity to love. Your mind is a great ally to your soul when it is directed by your heart and generated by the power of love. Your soul directs your mind through your intuitive consciousness and walks you into the lessons you need in order to build strength of character. The more your character develops, the more your soul reaches fulfillment. Your whole reason for being is to gain authority over your mind in the form of consciousness and use it to build strength of character to satisfy your soul. Your spirit is the 'energy' that comes from the Supreme Intelligence and from your soul to work as a connecting device between your mind and your heart. Your heart will provide you with everything you need via your feelings and emotions while you travel toward enlightenment and soulful evolution.

While your ultimate 'task' is to find your joy and share your love, there is nothing wrong with seeking and desiring wealth, setting goals, and gathering a cluster of nice things. In fact I encourage it, I just don't prioritise it above the need to love and create joy. The reason for this is that there is no fulfillment to be found in materialism. Your ego-mind is insatiable and will always desire 'more'. There will always be a better home, faster car, sexier partner, newer accessory, and more zeros to add to the end of your bank balance. True success, peace, and fulfillment are found within your soul, not your ego-mind. Your mind sees what it wants via the outside world whereas your soul commands what it wants via your inside world. Building strength of character and becoming more virtuous is like homeopathy for your soul. Your heart is your homeopath and the remedies it prescribes are virtues. There is a virtue to match every challenge you are faced with. You are an important part of the larger existence that vibrates on the frequency of love. The more character you build, the more your scope increases to love yourself and love others. Your ability to love fulfils your soul. Think for a minute on how it feels to make somebody laugh, to compliment, to help someone in need, to receive and give love to the people you are intimate and in close relationship with. There is nothing more concluding, rewarding, or gratifying.

No matter what you choose to 'want' in your life, be sure that it brings you joy, a joy that can be shared with others. Your soul commands companionship, and quality people to 'witness' your life and celebrate your successes. Success without others is not really success at all. Many people arrive at success and appear to have everything but they are lonely, isolated, and empty. A lonesome heart loses its desire to beat and breaks its contact with life. Your heart needs to be in communion with your soul, answering the call of inspiration, beating to the rhythm of your instincts, and discovering your divination regardless of the circumstances of your outside world, your current situation, or your immediate environment. The Supreme Intelligence reaches out to you so that amongst all the chaos in creation, all the distractions, disappointments, and disasters that occur, you can always find your way back to love. Love is the most influential force in the Universe. It is the only absolute power that is channelled to you and transmitted through you. Love is the reason you were created. I can only imagine that your very last breath in this lifetime is going to be accompanied by a memory of the people you have loved, the people who have loved you, and the brightness and purity of the ultimate love you are returning to.

One final note

I have a confession to make. I wrote this book more for me than for you. I needed a recipe to follow in order to remind myself how to live my life because I continue to struggle as much as the next person. Ripened virtues are my ideal and I strive to be everything I have suggested for you to be. Like I do, you can use this book as a reference and continue to choose from the list of virtues on a daily basis. Along with marrying a virtue to your next challenge, you can choose a different virtue every day to work on and ripen in yourself. When you complete the list, start again. Your soul work is never done. If you continue to do this, I guarantee your life will change, you will feel different, and you will never again be victim to anyone or anything. Developing strength of character and getting to know yourself, mind, body, and soul is all you need to do to improve yourself and enhance your life. Pay attention to where your mind takes you. What are your patterns? What causes you to feel 'low'? What triggers your anxiety and makes you lose faith? Take your mind to your heart and connect with how you feel about every possible topic. Listen to your body and trust your intuition. Your soul never lies to you and when you use the power of prayer, everything works out for the best.

In difficult times, pray hard. Life does not strive to 'teach you a lesson' or 'destroy you'. Life is a process that insists you grow and develop strength. For whatever reason, the Supreme Intelligence desires its soul, which is also your soul to experience being human in every possible way, to feel human love, to survive human pain, and to attain peace and fulfillment. I have no clue as to why this is. I only know that it is divinely desired and it is true because I feel the push and drive deep within me to love, evolve, and become what I can become while helping others along the way. You too have been chosen for this mission and to deny it will only cause you great pain and suffering. There is no force stronger than love and the Supreme Intelligence thrives on the love that is returned from all of us. Every time you feel the surge of love, the 'charge' of love pulsing through your veins and pounding through your body, that love is felt throughout the Universe. That love has the power to transform darkness, to supply hope for mankind, and to satisfy the collective soul of the Supreme Intelligence. Just as other people are targets for your love, you are targeted and loved despite your shadow and your weaknesses; in fact, you are loved even more for carrying the burden of these temptations while every day, despite your struggles and your challenges, choosing to become more love, light, and purity as you move fully into what you can become.

Two Ingredient Pancakes With Hot Pecan Sauce

Ingredients:

2 x perfectly ripe bananas, peeled, de-stringed, and mashed
2 x large eggs carefully cracked open

Method:

1. Blend or whisk the eggs and bananas to form a batter.
2. Place 1 tablespoon of coconut oil into a frying pan and pour the batter in a spiral to create a thin pancake.
3. Let the pancake cook for a few minutes on one side and then flip.
4. Serve with good quality Canadian maple syrup drizzled on top, a dollop of fresh cream, and some thinly sliced strawberries, or lash out and add some hot pecan sauce.

Hot Pecan Sauce:

Ingredients:

2 x 45g Bounty chocolate bars, chopped
1/2-cup cream
1/4-cup chopped pecans, toasted, plus extra to serve

Method:

In a saucepan, combine chopped Bounty bars and cream. Stir over a low heat until chocolate melts. Mix pecans through. Serve the pancakes topped with banana, extra pecans, a drizzle of sauce, and vanilla ice cream.

Make and share with love!

Noni Boon x

Printed in the United States
By Bookmasters